Another Pot of Coffee

Irena Milloy presents this second collection of her take on everyday issues encountered during her daily walk with God.

She lives in Cambridge with her husband and has for many years led quiet days and retreats, helping people to explore their own spirituality. She is also a Spiritual Director in the Diocese of Ely and enjoyed her time as a lay chaplain at the local hospital. She is an active member of the local ecumenical community.

Also by Irena Milloy

Coffee Pot Journal *first published 2008*

"Irena's 'Coffee Pot Journal' is a rare gem of a book, equally at home in the kitchen, where you can delve into it during those precious moments of peace over your favourite cup of coffee, or in the study, if you want to reflect more seriously on the practical wisdom that she shares through its pages. It's packed with my kind of theology - real, grounded and living. Irena has the rare knack of helping her readers to discern, in a truly Ignatian spirit, God in the everyday. I go to the Journal regularly, look forward to doing so and always come away better for it." *The Rev Scott Watts Worcestershire*

What a simple banquet. So writes Irena Milloy on October 16 in her book, *Coffee Pot Journal.* In church ministry for over thirty years, I appreciate how Irena discerns her faith in daily living then shares it in a refreshing way. Her insightful and moving reflections offer food for thought and feed the soul. Indeed, a simple banquet is offered on every page. May the feast continue.
The Reverend Jane Van Patter, The United Church of Canada

I look forward eagerly to the appearance of 'Another Pot of Coffee'. I still read the first one and depend on it to raise my spirits, remind me of how much I have to be thankful for or calm my heart. .....The thing I love best about it is that your musings cover so very many of the everyday things that we experience in daily life. Though I don't chase chickens, it is the mundane everyday things in life that enrich us or puzzle or distress us or make us thankful and they are all covered in one place or another in the book. I hope that the new one will continue that theme.   *Barbara Swift   Chicago*

Irena has a gift for bringing God into the busyness of our everyday lives. In her daily reflections, she helps us to bring our worries, our joys, our questions to the throne of grace. Those quiet moments with a cup of coffee and Irena's thoughts, prayers and poems create an oasis of peace and prayerfulness each day. Can't wait for "Another Pot of Coffee" to be in print!
Margaret Whewell   Portsoy Aberdeenshire

It really was the Christmas present that lasted all year.
Helen Drew Auckland NZ

Another Pot of Coffee

Continuing a Journey in Faith

by

Irena Milloy

Avon Court Publishing

First Edition – May 2017

ISBN 978-0-9559302-1-8

Published in the UK
by Avon Court Publishing
1 Ambrose Way, Cambridge CB24 9US

Additional copies may ordered from the author at:
avoncourt@themilloys.co.uk

Another Pot of Coffee

"Can I have another cup of coffee please?" Readers of Irena Milloy's *Coffee Pot Journal* have been asking that question, ever since they finished her record of "A Year's Journey in Faith". Now she has brewed them a fresh pot, full of new "poems, prayers, meditations, and musings". Irena experiences the presence of God in everyday events, very much as Brother Lawrence did in the seventeenth century, and she invites us to share her experience: to give thanks to God with her for his gifts, and to discover more of his truth in unexpected places.

For those of us who are privileged to number Irena among our friends, nothing is more enjoyable than sitting down with her to share a cup of coffee. Readers who enjoyed her first journal will be eager to accept the invitation to join her once again at her kitchen table and learn from her down-to-earth spirituality.

Morna Hooker

Professor Morna Hooker is Lady Margaret's Professor of Divinity Emerita, University of Cambridge

Many thanks to dear Peter for his patient listening
and constant support

January 1st

At the start of this New Year
Make me to know your ways O Lord,
Show me your paths.
Lead me in your truth and teach me,
For you are the God of my salvation;
For you I wait
all day long.   Ps 25 : 4-5

January 2nd

My mother used to say that the Lord never sent more than your shoulders
could bear but she would then add in some tone 'He must think I have a
very broad back!'
Now as I grouse at what I have to do, some of it self-inflicted, well most of
it self-inflicted, I'm thinking about Matthew 11: 25-30 where Jesus said:
'Come to me all you who are weary and heavy burdened and I will give you
rest. Take my burden upon you and learn from me; for I am gentle and
humble in heart and you will find rest for your souls. For my yoke is easy
and my burden light'.
And I'm thinking that half the 'burdens' I'm carrying I have no need to, they
are there because I haven't had the sense to put them down. They are there
because I seem to think the world will stop if I am not physically involved in
the machinations of village life, church life, family life; what's going on at
the gym, in the next village or in Canada with my sister!
Oh Lord no sympathy needed, it's all self-inflicted.

January 3rd

Pomp and Circumstance? Pomp and Pomposity? In thinking about this title for a study day I have been asked to prepare, I watched some suggested clips from various solemn occasions, two of which were the Pope's inauguration and the inauguration of the Archbishop of Canterbury, both taking place in the same week in 2013. Glorious occasions of acknowledgment that God is still very much at the heart of so much of our world despite the desolation and abandonment we often feel.

At the same time as working on this project for Easter, we have just celebrated Christmas, when Jesus arrived with none of the trappings of the above. Whose mark on the world will be the greater?

Interesting that the totally humble Babe of Bethlehem, without any drum or fanfare, achieved what no other, before or since has.

It isn't such a big leap from Pomp to pomposity; Lord let me give the former to you and beware of the second in myself.

January 4th

I just read that George Orwell wrote:

'They sleep safely in their beds because rough men stand ready in the night to visit violence on those who would do them harm'.

Wow, what a terrifying thought, that as I close my eyes on another day I am surrounded by an army of moustachioed bandoliers intent on making guerrilla warfare out of my night's sleep! I much prefer to have turned my thoughts to the childhood prayer,

'Matthew, Mark, Luke and John, bless this bed that I lie on

Four corners to my bed, four angels round my head,

One to watch and one to pray

And two to bear my soul away'...................not that I am planning the latter just yet!

January 5th

'I was only going to say that heaven did not seem to be my home; and I broke my heart with weeping to come back to earth; and the angels were so angry that they flung me out into the middle of the heath on the top of Wuthering Heights; where I woke sobbing for joy'
Catherine Earnshaw 'Wuthering Heights'

Wow, this is so powerful and heartbreaking in that it is the antithesis to the aspirations most of us think about when contemplating heaven.

January 6th

Epiphany, the official end to Christmas, the baptism of Jesus and the arrival of the Magi when Melchior, Casper and Balthasar brought symbolic gifts pre-figuring the Life of Christ. Gold representing his royal standing, frankincense his divine birth and myrrh his mortality.
All he wants from me is my faithful trust.

January 7th

I am beginning to get a bit fed up of being preached at! Not from the pulpit in church but from the soap box of the 'pontificators'.

I know they are following their beliefs but am I alone in being tired of being told how to recycle my rubbish, how to improve the insulation of my home, how to build a more productive compost heap...... on and on they write or drone, expounding the latest theory in 'green fertiliser', animal safe slug deterrents, earth closets over flushing lavatories, biodegradable this, ozone friendly the other......... Oh please give me a break! I used to be so fired up to every new initiative for the planet, every philosophy on how to build the new Utopia. Then I realised that I couldn't do it all according to the idealistic dictum.

All I can do is try. All I can do is my best. I do recycle my rubbish, but my council doesn't take the same stuff as the one where my daughter lives, so where does mine go and where does her rubbish go? We only live 30 miles apart. I compost as much as I can because I'm a gardener, although, the plastic wrapper is marked bio-degradable I am not to put it in my bin – then where!

Is there any way we Christians could be more proactive in spreading **our** message or would it just be received with the same ennui as all the others? How can we challenge ourselves to get out there with a message of joyful deliverance from sin? A message of hope and unconditional love? How can we get some enthusiasm and commitment in ourselves to build the New Jerusalem? Probably by just 'doing', no soap boxes, no loud hailers, just being ready to share the love of God when the opportunity arises - instead of thinking about it afterwards.

January 8th

Am I a Christian Apologist?   Yes.
I find myself constantly defending the faith in discussions about the apparent mess the church is making of things, the mess the church seems to be in, the mess the wishy-washy doctrinaires are making……and on and on.
What matters? What should I be saying?
Let's get back to the one basic fact on which everything – everything, has to predicated,

Jesus. Jesus is Lord.

January 9th

Another tear stained face on the news today and
another woman I haven't even met to pray for.
Another example of man's inhumanity to man
and man's complete and utter disregard for the women
and children in his world.
Another rant as I hurl impotent words
like sharpened spears into the ceiling
and another realization that I can't tell
her I'm feeling for her.
The Red Cross says they'll use my gift
to ease her agony and give her a lift with coping
but mine is the easy way out not done with grace
as I lick the envelope and forget her face until
another tear stained apparition fills the screen
and another woman I've never seen starts to
look like the last one.

January 10th

'I love you'
I tell the family all the time, at least I think I do.
I tell my Husband all the time, at least I think I do.
I hope I tell my special friends how very precious they are to me and that I love them,
at least I hope I do.
Do I ever tell Jesus? Do I ever say, 'Jesus I love you'?
I sing it in hymns of praise at church but when I am spending quiet time with my Lord do I ever say:
'Jesus I love you'?
People of an older generation wouldn't hold with all this talk of 'love', they would probably say it was sloppy, but we all need to hear it don't we?
I know that my appreciation of His love for me is confined by my pitiful human understanding but I'll just tell Him more often that I love Him.

January 11th

I won't say 'I know how you're feeling'
I won't say 'I know where you hurt'
I can't take the burden from you
I can't make it all go away.
But I can lift you up to my Jesus
And ask Him to soothe all your pain
And hold you and wrap you in safety
Until you feel steady again.
I know you don't think He listens
You aren't even sure if he's there
So allow me to bring you before Him
To the warmth at the hearth of his Heart.

January 12th

'Life can only be lived in the present time', said Dennis Potter the playwright as he faced death from multiple cancers.
Do we need to face death before we truly begin to appreciate each new day?
Do we really need to be reminded to live each day as if it were the last?
We all know people who seem to be more memory than present, who can only harp back to how things were, to how things were done, to how things were made, said, built, cooked; and don't even start on how children were raised………..
Memory is good, memories are precious and give form to the shape of family and society but if we are to stay alive, to live, we must move onwards, we can't be stuck in the past or we will fossilise and be dead, long before we need to be.

January 13th

In the light of yesterday's thought I realised that there were some things I need to get on with, not because I have lived in the past but I can be a procrastinator. This is a big problem because in putting off what needs to be done I have maybe missed the opportunity to do some important things.

I missed the chance to apologise to someone, who I had inadvertently hurt, leaving it for so long that the time never did come...or so I explained to myself!

I have let friendships fizzle because I didn't make enough effort to stay in touch, not deliberately but because I was always 'going to'.

I'm always going to build in more quiet time to be with the Lord but perhaps next week.

This is not a confessional but an acknowledgement that I really do need live like Dennis Potter and countless others whose days are numbered,

'in the present time'.

January 14th

I won't recognise myself tomorrow. I was given a free sample of a new anti-wrinkle treatment today and it says that applied overnight the ingredients will have time to re-energise and restore my skin by 10 years. I think I should stay awake to watch it happen!
What a load of baloney and the sad thing is I accepted it so gratefully and gracefully. Once home I read the back of the little box to affirm the promise and directions for use. Yes, apply to clean face!
I took something, in which I had little faith, willingly and with perhaps a grain of hope for some star dust to help halt nature.
Why when we try to share our faith and the promise of eternal life are we not similarly so readily received?
Why does the expectation offered by the Gospel not raise as much anticipation?

January 15th

How literally are we supposed to take the Bible?
Proverbs 23 v12 tells us:
'Don't hesitate to discipline a child, a good spanking won't kill him. As a matter of fact it might save his life.' Good News Bible
'Withhold not correction from a child for if thou beatest him with the rod he shall not die.' King James Bible
'Do not withhold discipline from a boy take the stick to him and save him from death.' The revised English Bible
As with so many verses there is now a code of behaviour and an appropriacy of going about things which has moved away from the direction of the 'good book'. I don't think that a little tap in some circumstances leads to crippling psychological problems in later life nor do I think that beating with a stick, hand or anything else is ever acceptable but having just been subjected to some extremely 'high spirited' youngsters with no sense of time place or thought for others, I am moved to get physical.

January 16th

I want a dog to walk.

I no longer have my dear old black lab and I miss her. I don't miss the mess from her having a good shake as soon as she entered the house, splattering the walls and kitchen cupboards with a chic shade of pond water and making the house smell the same. I don't miss the balls of hair gently dancing like tumbleweed across the floor, usually in the draft from the door I am opening to visitors. I don't miss clearing up after her in the garden.

I do miss having a dog to walk on a glorious day like today has been. I went out anyway and enjoyed the cold clear air, striding out to raise a sweat and pulse rate but I felt like there was something missing and there was, there was no one to talk to. I really did a lot of talking things through with her on a walk. No one to argue with me, no one to even really hear or care, but another pair of ears which made articulating somehow more real and useful than just thinking.

Dear old Tilly I do miss you so much.

January 17th

How many folk have sailed through life unhampered by trials and heartbreak?

It's easy to feel like one's own suffering is much more of a tribulation than anything anyone else has experienced when the chips are down and the hurting is totally invasive and no amount of rationale soothes. The thing is, that as I think about any group of friends whether in church, the gym or any other meeting point, I can identify individuals with whom I am familiar and know that behind practically every front door there has been pain. No one has been trouble free, No one has escaped some time of deep worry and or sadness. No one has escaped the scars of their experience.

Where are the treatment centres? Where have people gone to have their wounds bound up?

It would be glib to immediately think of church, in fact for a lot of people, sadly, that has been where the hurt started. Where then? Where can one get the best treatment?

The ears of a loving, listening presence. No words, no sympathetic utterances of 'understanding', just someone in whom supreme trust can be relied on to keep vigil and absorb anything of the incoming pain with open acceptance.

It is through experiences collective and personal that society is enabled to be the hospitallers of an individual or community, and through compassionate acknowledgement of one's own hurt, that one can be used for the good of others.

Lord teach me just to listen and not to feel obliged to have an answer.

January 18th

'And the Lord said unto Moses'.

My mother and her friend, whom I called Auntie Nellie, used to say this with comic timing and boring predictability when as children we asked for anything or about anything. I never knew what the Lord had said to Moses that could have ever have had any relevance to the request for an extra hour playing out time, or whether my best friend could come for tea or if we could have some water and biscuits for a picnic. I do remember though that I did, a few years later, try it on for myself after being asked about homework....

'And the Lord said unto Moses' I threw over my shoulder as I hopped it upstairs, waiting for the reprimand, though it didn't come. Poised on the top stair I looked back at my mother who had followed me into the hall and she was smiling wryly. With a shake of her head she seemed to be saying 'it's a fair cop' as I headed off to my room and she to the kitchen.

Curious to get to the root of this family 'bon mot' I turned to my biblical encyclopaedia and found that there were so many quotes beginning with... 'And the Lord said unto Moses' that I have a thought. Perhaps Methodist Sunday School children in the early 20th century, being read great chunks of the Bible week in, week out, three times a Sunday, latched onto this phrase in the way that today's youngsters use colloquialisms such as 'yeh whatever' and 'aint it though', but then took the words through to adulthood and found them useful in placating their pestering children.

January 19th

Sign in a physio's office:
'There aren't enough crutches in the world for all the lame excuses I hear'
Lord, do I see you and my faith as a crutch? Do I use you and my faith in this way? Do I, almost with familiar nonchalance, just accept you and your love for me and your support for me? I am thinking of the 'familiarity breeds contempt' phrase as I write and I am ashamed even to acknowledge the thought. God forbid that in knowing you are closer to me than I am to myself, that I in anyway, show you a lack of due reverence.
I know I do, which is why I offer up such lame excuses for why I am not more faithful and earnest in seeking out time to be with you.
I am so sorry.

January 20th

'Live the life you live, not the life of your dreams'. I need to think on this.

January 21st

What a strange day. It was fine and quite sunny so I went into the garden to do a bit of tiding up and to see what was coming through – lots as it happens – suddenly, with the extra warmth. The robins were fighting for my attention and yes, I know that in theory they are territorial little chaps and so there's usually only one per plot but we have actually got two that we see regularly and at the same time. Anyway, they were shouting their wares, each one trying to sound more impatient than the other and eventually got my undivided attention so I looked up. Up past them, well up, in fact to where the clouds and the sunshine were also vying for supremacy. The clouds had blown up into dark, bruised pillows, mustering for a fight and the sun, although about to be consumed by them was making a brilliant spotlight to herald their incredible majesty. I was quite awe struck as I watched the gradual movement from sunlight to strange light to downpour and I dived into the shed.

Taking the opportunity to tidy up some pots I had knocked over earlier I begin to scrabble on my hands and knees around and under the potting table, scooping them up along with dried leaves and the general detritus of a working shed floor when I felt, rather than saw, something small, fast and furry jump for freedom. Of course, that made jump too and I dropped the handful of rubbish, pots and all and sat back on my heels, heart pounding. Poor little field mouse, I had completely destroyed her nest, scared her more than she scared me and left us both feeling quite vulnerable. Two sides of the coin, like the sky, like the robins. I feel there's something in all this but I am too tired to ponder further.

January 22nd

I don't think I am supposed to think too much about all my experiences of yesterday apart from to acknowledge that I am a part of a truly wonderful world. I could hypothesize all day about the allegory behind the cloud formations and I could beat myself into a pulp for breaking up the mouse's house. I could draw parallels from two war lord robins living in seeming harmony. But I won't.
Lord thank you for yesterday and for my sight.

January 23rd

Why don't I claim the promises of Jesus more often?
'My God shall supply all your needs according to his riches in glory by Christ Jesus'. Philippians 4: 19
'God has promised that His grace is sufficient for us'. II Corinthians 12: 9
He has made provision for our salvation by His grace through faith.
Ephesians 2 :8
It is through an obedient faith that we have access into the grace of God according to Romans 5: 2.

All my **needs,** not my wants or wishes
His grace is sufficient, as proved to Paul with his thorn in the flesh (the messenger from Satan). God's power is strongest when we are weak and as long as we, in our weakness, turn and cling to his promise we will deepen our awareness of the greater power and receive grace.
Salvation through faith. Salvation = redemption, deliverance, rescue, escape; that's what salvation actually means.
We are **justified** by faith, we have peace with God, and we have gained access by faith into this grace in which we now stand.

Lord make me worthy to claim your promises and to stand before you in honest nakedness.

January 24th

Accept surprises
that upset your plans,
shatter your dreams,
bring a new turn to your day
and, who knows, your life.
It is not fate.
Leave the Father free
Himself to weave
the pattern of your days.

Helda Camara

January 25th

In every relationship there is a gardener and a flower.
I heard this on the radio in a debate the other day and it was like one of those annoying tunes, *ear worms*, they're called, that plague you for the rest of the day.
 I kept thinking about my various relationships and whether I was the gardener or the flower. Some are very clearly defined in these terms, some I feed and others I am fed but, the more deeply I thought about it the more I thought that most of my relationships are a mix of the two rolls. Sometimes I am the one doing the looking after and other times I need the care, the mothering, the leading. And I think that in this symbiosis lies the more total relationship, the one with the greater trust, the one with the joy of sharing and revealing, or nurturing and being nurtured.
I think I will be analysing my relationships more closely for a while, though all are precious.

January 26th

'In all things God works for the good of those who love him, who have been called according to his purpose'.   Romans 8: 28

Well the purpose was that I had forgotten I was 'on chapel flowers' and at 11pm on Friday night realised that I would have to be up very early to go and buy flowers and drive to College to get the arrangement in place for the weekend services. There was no time to raid the garden for artistic greenery or twigs with a Hogarth curve about them, there was no time to do anything 'til morning when I would have to get into gear very quickly.

So, awake half the night, I gave up on bed at 6.30 a.m. and hastily left to go via the large 24-hour supermarket to buy as many flowers as it would take to make it look like I had meant to do this presentation all along. Traffic! Lots of it, already cars of other early birds getting in my way. I could almost hear God laughing at the lather I was getting into.... remember Irena, 'In all things God works for the good of those who love him'.... this verse just came from nowhere and brought a semblance of order and serenity to my panic.

I was at the supermarket by 7.15 and in chapel by 8am doing my arrangement, well ahead of anyone seeking a quiet place.

God works in all things, and although in this instance I could be accused of trivialising Paul's words as he presented the Gospel to the Romans, I hope I may be forgiven for using them to instil some peace into my self-inflicted muddle.

And I will, always, now make a bigger note in my diary of the chapel flower rota!

January 27th

'Holding onto anger is like grasping a hot coal with the intent of throwing it at someone else; you are the one who gets burnt' Buddha.

On boy, I know this to be true. How often have I passed my anger and or frustration on in the next situation only to cause an even bigger upset by my awful behaviour? And this is then usually compounded by the recipient of my ill grace being generous and forgiving and therefore leaving me feeling even more disgusted with myself.

Then, another 'enlightenment' moment, last night when my dear Buddhist friend completed the teaching by adding that the way to assuage your anger with someone is to send them a present, an unconditional gift! Now that *is* original to me.

I am a long way from attaining peace, Buddhist or Christian.

January 28th

'There are no mistakes. You might do it differently next time, but that's because you did it this way this time. Even if you say too much this, too little that, it's you and be pleased to be yourself'.

I found these words in a bread making book lent to me by my son-in-law, who is a cracking bread-maker; I am still very much a novice but these prophetic words are from a compendium called Tassajara Bread Book.

How often do I beat myself up because I haven't got something quite right, quite perfect and how often does it actually make much difference? I know I must keep trying, but it does become negative and defeating if we don't occasionally give ourselves a pat on the back for trying.

January 29th

I know there will never peace in my lifetime. I know there will never be peace ever. I know it because we are human and humans are so deeply flawed.

Rumi, a Persian poet of the 13th century wrote:

'Out beyond ideas of wrong-doing and right-doing, there is a field. I'll meet you there'.

I think he is talking about heaven. Where else could this field be? Where else could there be a place beyond opinion, beyond ego, beyond self?

And, who, this side of heaven would consider themselves so utterly without guile that they would dare to go there?

January 30th

I wonder if I could get a subsidy from the EU towards my bird food bill. They bring enormous pleasure and we enjoy the 'one-upmanship' of what and how many we have seen. But, having just been to stock up on seeds, wild bird and Niger, peanuts and fat balls, I am close to spending more than some families live on and that makes me very uncomfortable. And yes, my thought of a subsidy was flippant.

Does God want me to do this? Why am I doing it? Am I doing it to help God's creatures as part of my duty to conserving nature, or what, or why?

No, it is a purely selfish decision to do something which brings us delight. Are we making the birds lazy loading up our bird feeders and tables? There are differing opinions, even among the cognoscenti. Furthermore, why do I feel that I should analyse and over evaluate every last thing I do? I am in danger of boring myself to death.

Dear God, you know what's in my mind and heart even before I do, so give me a sense of balance I pray.

January 31st

Timeless night..................... How long night takes to get to be day when you're lying awake worrying and sore. Mine is a minor issue in the greater scheme of things; a bit of back ache and worry that I won't be as fit as I could be to go away with friends which will involve some long walks. What about the length of night though when there really is something to worry about and the pain is a genuine issue, maybe even a terminal issue? Then the night must truly be interminable. And yes, we are blithely told 'don't count sheep, talk to the shepherd' but in a night that stretches without form or markers, words are inadequate and deeply ineffectual. Dawn will come, another day will come for most of us and for most of us a more positive state of mind will warm the chills away. For some though the day will only bring an impending dread of the night yet to come and living in this fear, living in this paralysing and all-consuming fear is beyond my comprehension.

February 1st

'The clown is the mirror of our society'
Is this true? The great big make-up smile, painted on to cover up the sadness behind.
Where is the smile on the face of society right now? Is not misery, filth, dishonesty, disappointment, shared for all to see?
Is not society now washing its laundry in public to an alarming degree; no longer able or even content to cope quietly behind the scenes with its troubles; no longer able to behave with a shred of dignity, to preserve the sensibilities and feelings of people whose lives have been turned over by a tragedy?
We tread a fine line between wanting to know and needing to know. I tread a fine line when I buy a magazine with an 'in-depth' interview headlined. I tread a fine line when I read a salacious report about something I really don't *need* to know about. I then appease my conscience by claiming I'm just keeping up with current affairs. Next thing I feel cross with myself and sad at my weakness but hey, I will be a clown, I will step out with my made-up public face and try to bring something good to the day.

February 2nd

Heavenly Father
Thank God you don't give
out in due measure
to what I
put in.
Thank God
your vision is
beyond my narrow tunnel
of sight.
Praise and thanksgiving
that your blessings
eclipse even my most
generous act judged only in the
frailest human terms.
Praise and wonder at your total
forgiveness for sincere
but hurried and
forgotten apology.
Heartfelt trust in your power
which underwrites me.

February 3rd

I will sing of the Lord's great love for ever; with my mouth I will make your faithfulness known through all generations. I will declare that your love stands firm for ever, that you established your faithfulness in Heaven itself .

Ps. 89: 1-2

February 4th

I'm sitting here at the kitchen table thinking 'those windows need cleaning and the curtains could do with washing….oh and I mustn't forget….and I really must…. and I ought to….and the joy with which I got up a couple of hours ago has evaporated into an obligatory, rather disgruntled mush.
For goodness sake woman, shake yourself up. Look through the windows, beyond a bit of dust, away from cobwebs and curtains. Look! Look outside. Look at the sky, the clouds their shapes and colours, the trees, their shapes and colours, the bricks in the wall opposite, their shades and surfaces.
Gerard Manley Hopkins wrote 'The world is changed with the grandeur of God'
God gave us eyes to see Him.
Now, get on with it. Look!

February 5th

The reading today in my bible notes is
'I live now, not with my own life but with the life of Christ who lives in me'
Gal. 2: 20

I feel that's almost more responsibility than I felt when I was pregnant carrying my unborn children and the implications of it on a day to day, hour by hour basis. In fact, I find it makes me immobile in case I do something wrong or inadvertently hurt it, that parcel of 'Christ's life in me'.
My reaction is the antithesis of the promised power from having that 'life' inside me. I don't feel empowered, I don't feel ready or worthy to be on the receiving end of such a gift. I feel like I should keep very still and not jar or upset the special life within me. I must have read this verse a hundred times before and it has never had this impact on me in the past.
What am I to make of my reaction?
I have gone back to Galatians and read again the promises which Paul explains and yes, this gift of 'life' is in me and I am sanctified by that and not by living according to the 'law'. So, for me I will always strive to remember that my body is the temple of the Holy Spirit but then claim my loyalty points and live a spirit filled life clothed in the armour of God. From the inside out as it were.

February 6th

I so wish I'd done more piano practice.

I can hear the grown-ups telling me how much I would regret not practicing enough and OK, they were right. I do.

I can do enough to pick out a few nursery rhymes or hymns but I really wish I could just sit down and play with competency and flair. I had the chance and I blew it.

I also had the chance whilst in the youth club attached to my local church, of learning more bible verses by heart for inter-church competitions, and I thought it was just so very boring and un-trendy.

How I wish now, that I had those verses engraved on my mind, like the poems I learned and can still recite with ease. I can remember a few and have tried over the years to commit others to memory but I wish I had done it when I had the opportunity and mental acuity.

Lord how frustrating it must be, watching us loose or misuse our talents and opportunities.

February 7th

'Decisions are made by those who turn up'.
I heard this quotation on the radio yesterday but without any accreditation so I started to research it and ended up in a quagmire of slithering by various goodly bodies who all seemed to claim it as their own.
So, I am not claiming any originality but am still very moved by the sentiment.
In fact, I'm a bit uncomfortable because I so often feel aggrieved by a process or plan put in place without anyone consulting me. I take umbrage at decisions made on my behalf concerning community issues, village plans, transport changes, traffic flows, church service styles, changes to the processes which make my life liveable.
When did I last attend a village council meeting? Not for a long time.
When did I last offer to go on the Parochial Church Council? Not for a long time.
Perhaps the quotation should read:
'Decisions are made by those who turn up - so put up or shut up'.
That's me told.

February 8th

After making myself uncomfortable yesterday – the truth does hurt sometime – I heard the wonderful song 'My Sweet Lord' on the radio. George Harrison's love song written to Lord Krishna at the height of the Beatle's time with the Maharishi Yogi and during their search for inner peace and contentment. It was at No 1 for 5 weeks in January 1971.
I can't begin to imagine the impact of a recording called 'My Sweet Lord Jesus', then or now.

February 9th

'Pointless', I watch it and I enjoy trying to answer the questions, getting the most obscure answer in order to have as few points as possible.
I don't know why but I was thinking about what is or isn't pointless and realised one **huge** thing, our faith sets us up for the ultimate win win situation because we have to be pointless to get into heaven.
No amount of learning, no amount of money, no amount of goods and chattels, no number of good works, committees or fund raising will get us there. The only thing will be a heart for Jesus and a prayer that His grace will be sufficient.

February 10th

The Good Samaritan took pity on the injured man.

The Good Samaritan was the image on my hospital badge, presented to me on qualification to State Registered Nurse status. I use the word status deliberately because there was a real feeling of change from what I had been before to another place, another state. A State Registered Nurse. I was so proud, we all were and acutely aware of the compassion and professionalism expected from us. But 'pity' we were taught was not a positive reaction to any situation that would present itself. It seemed I had always understood the word incorrectly. Pity doesn't mean to feel 'sorry for' as in apologetic or in a superior way as the empty phrase 'I'm sorry for your trouble'. Pity means to **feel** 'sorrow', a recognition of a place where support, help, guidance of another human being is what is needed. Pity = to feel sorrow, not sorry.

Lord forgive me for all the times without number I have said the words but thought thankfully that it wasn't me in that situation.

February 11th

Yesterday's piece made me look, uncomfortably, at the very flawed way I have so often tossed off a platitude to someone and I cringe.

Open my eyes, I dare to see
beyond the ironed patina of presentation.
Open my eyes, I dare to see
inside the closed-up cupboard, the clutter
and chaos of life.
Open my eyes, I dare to see the tears and blood
of pain so long ignored.
Open my ears, I dare to hear
the unsaid sadness silting up of a
soul in pain.
Open my ears, I dare to hear
the hate and harm of bewildered faith
yearning for rightness
and restoration.
And in my openness
and in my daring
may my pity be the love of Christ
reaching outwards.

February 12th

I'm really missing the dog. It is a gloriously cold, bright day and if there was still the expectant, trusting gaze of my dear mutt behind the door I would, without demur be off for a lovely walk by the river. But there isn't the incentive and I feel less likely to give myself the permission needed to stop work and go off on my own. Part of it, I realise has been the security of having a dog with me, though goodness knows what she would have done if a situation had arisen, also exercising her was a part of a routine which changed with her passing.

The thing that has suffered hugely though is that I have lost a lovely and valuable prayer time.

Now, that must be the best reason yet for getting back out there, with or without a dog.

February 13th

He that believeth shall not make haste.   Isaiah 28: 16

Clearly things were a bit different in Isiah's day then!

Haste is the determining factor by which I live my life, or it seems that way. Clockwatching, not enough hours in the day, being pulled in all directions, the treadmill of life has been cranked up several notches.

I remember the chap next door retiring when I was 16. Mr and Mrs Brown assumed a completely different lifestyle, slower and somehow more dignified. They gardened their precious roses, went for days out to the coast for lunch, walked to the village shops and back, with time to talk to anyone they met and always with time to ask my sisters and I about our plans and dreams.

Now my friends are beginning to retire and the world has changed. They haven't got time to stand and stare, they haven't got a day to themselves, they haven't got the finances in many cases, to support all that needs their support. Elderly and often infirm parents, in a role reversal not considered, now need a vast amount of care whist at the other end of the family table, children are needing physical help with their offspring. My 'retired' friends are anything but and I worry about them.

He that believeth shall not make haste! Well Isaiah, there ain't no alternative that I can see; only a thankfulness that in faith and with the Grace of the Lord they will cope.

February 14th

What Isaiah did go onto say was that we should still our hearts and minds though, looking at yesterday's thought there doesn't seem to be much opportunity for that.

The 'haste' will be forever present but where is our soul's attitude to the hurly burly? Are we insidiously driving a wedge deeper and deeper into the crevasse between soul and maker? Am I?

Our role model is Jesus. He lived his short life to the full. He did though take himself away from the greedy throng to have time with his heavenly father God.

In living our lives today we constantly miss the essential things and in missing those we end up in a downward spiral of struggle, a vortex of grasp and grab. STOP, stop and evaluate. Go through the days and assess the how and the why. How many of the impositions are being made through a deeper misunderstanding of need. A need to be needed. In that state who becomes the dependant and who is the depended upon? In that state we are surely not contributing to the glory of Christ but actually ever widening the chasm to be filled with more obligations.

STOP, STOP now and take time to be with your heavenly Father God who loves you and wants to hold you to himself for a while. Listen to yourself Irena.

February 15th

Faithful God, you tend to the needs of your whole creation. You hear every prayer – the ones we speak out loud and the ones deep in our hearts. Forgive me for times when I have turned to unhealthy, unhelpful solutions to a problem. Forgive me for times when I have been consumed by my worries instead of openly accepting your grace. Strengthen my trust in you, God. Forgive me and empower me to walk humbly with you. In Jesus name. Amen.

February 16th

It is still winter. It is still cold.
It is still dark for much of the day and I am a little bit tired of it all. No, I'm sick to death of it.
So, I've had a brainwave. I'm going to get a few friends together, starting here in my home and have a favourite film afternoon. Then maybe next week we could go to someone else to share their favourite DVD. A cup of tea or coffee, good company and sharing, what could be better.
I'm off to start phoning round.

February 17th

The chap on the radio was talking about 'Growing in faith' and seemed to be basing it on a quite charismatic view point which set me thinking. There might well have been a Damascene conversion to kick start the journey. There may be sudden revelations of God's purpose for individuals after periods of quiet contemplation. For most though, the eureka moment is not an experience understood but rather the quiet, deepening faith which establishes itself at the core of the believer as that person learns to trust God.

'Growing in faith' is incremental as we step out, trusting in the truth of the Gospel message we will be lead onwards and inwards to a place that we will come to recognise as our God space and our spiritual core. We will also come to realise that the more we can take into that God space the more it can hold.

February 18th

Freewill must be limited, ideally by ourselves, otherwise freewill and all its amazing benefit becomes selfishness.

February 19th

Thinking and writing as I often do, about the practice of prayer and praying, I came across this wonderful encapsulation of the subject from the Priest, missionary Jean Vanier.

'Prayer is God. It is the movement of God to man and man to God, the rhythm of encounter and response. It is a living encounter with a living God'.

I wish I had found this several thousand words and chapters ago.

February 20th

On the subject of short and to the point observations, the Victorian preacher Spurgeon wrote:

'Anxiety doesn't empty tomorrow of its trouble
but drains today of its strength'. Amen.

February 21st

I have found flowers in my garden in a corner that I had given up on. What a gift!
A dark, shady, cold corner that I have never tried to cultivate. The miracle is that a bird showed it to me. No I am not going dotty! I was walking down the garden to go and get some leeks for dinner, the only vegetables left to pick, and I heard a rustling in the leaves. I thought it was perhaps a rabbit, the bane of my husband's life and so I wanted to be able to see it and report back. But no; there, scratching about, was a beautiful blackbird. I know he was looking for grubs but to me it seemed as though he was trying to liberate the stunning blue miniature irises so they could be appreciated and have their moment of glory. I have no idea how they got there but it shamed me into thinking that nowhere in a garden is a waste of space. It also showed me, yet again, that someone much bigger that I am is control, even in the unloved places, perhaps more so in the unloved places.

February 22nd

I did it. Remember a few days ago I bemoaned the lack of a dog to take for a walk, to give myself permission to go out? Well, it has been a truly glorious day and almost warm enough to be without a coat, so I set off and did a long loop through the village, and out across the fields in the opposite direction to usual. Two things were apparent, the first was how different the same walk seemed going the other way, seen from a different perspective and in a different light and secondly, how affirmed I felt when I arrived home.
All of it was somewhat tempered when my husband said he didn't like the thought of me doing that walk on my own so far from any help, should I have needed it, even with my mobile phone. Now I feel rather selfish that I have caused him some anxiety. Oh what a juxtaposition of feelings and opinions.

February 23rd

The Benedictine Rule begins:
'Now is the hour to rise from sleep, let us open our eyes, let us hear with attentive ears and run while we have the light of life'.
How might this call challenge me each day before I succumb to its pressures and situations?
'Now is the hour' – Now is the time, the immediacy of this command. Procrastination is not an option, another half hour under the duvet is not on.
Let is **open** our eyes – not just from sleep but as new sight, new clarity of purpose and understanding. Challenging the way one looks at assumptions, bigotries, self-absorption.
Hear, listen, with **attentive** ears Don't just listen passively but hear, really hear, comprehend and discern the Gospel message pertinent to life here and now. Sort the wheat from the chaff of all that demeans, diminishes or disassembles a Gospel life.
Let us **run –** not walk, time is of the essence. Do it now, no more postponements.
And all before breakfast.

February 24th

Another reading from Isaiah in my Daily Notes today and the more I read the more I find answers to so many of my conundrums on faith in this large book. This today though is a real leap of faith if I think about it regarding a colleague who has just learned that she is very poorly, maybe terminal.
'Though the mountains be shaken and the hills be removed, yet my unfailing love for you will not be shaken nor my covenant of peace be removed'.
I cannot go to her with this even though she has some faith. It is too soon for her to get beyond the devastating news, but I can hold her close and bind her in this promise in prayer.   Is. 54: 10

February 25th

Why is leading one's self always harder than leading and encouraging others? On the face of it and with the inherent arrogance of man we can kid ourselves that we are right whatever the subject. If, however we try to see ourselves as God might see us then of course we would be hesitant to step out at all in case we let him down. Never mind the worry, we are all much more comfortable giving advice than taking it. Encouraging others rather than ourselves, seems to give us the ultimate opt out clause. I need to give myself a nudge in many directions and need to get a grip of myself. Affirmation is OK.

February 26th

The Quiet Garden Movement newsletter has just arrived. As always it is full of beautiful thought and sentiment, upholding and salving hurt spirits and minds.

In my old garden I had prayer corners and quiet places where people there for a quiet day or retreat could go, alone, to be helped by mother nature, to find some calm. My new plot is much, much smaller but there are a couple of places where the overarching branches of a tree and a scented corner provide safe harbour to be still, to hear the still small voice, to wait up on the Lord.

Jesus said, 'Come with me by yourselves and get some rest'.   Mark 6: 31

Thank you for my garden Lord.

February 27th

The *Three Presents*, not beautifully wrapped boxes with bows and streamers though.
Henri Nouwen highlights the three-in-one journey of being *'present'* to ourselves, *'present'* with and for others and *'present'* to God. All these are gifts of great merit but how does this affect the me. There is a lot to think about here. Maybe I should get out into one of my garden prayer corners and wait on the Lord.

February 28th

This morning
I take time to be with my Lord.
To place myself before His gaze and
confess all that is without beauty in myself.
I beg that He will, through the power of the Holy Spirit
forgive and heal me,
direct my day and lead me forward.
I ask for the grace to know Jesus more intimately
to love him more intensely
and to follow Him more closely.   Amen.

February 29th

A free day. A day Leap Year was 'invented' back in the first century BC, when Julius Caesar and his team of astronomers noticed that their 365-day Roman calendar had somehow slipped out of sync with the seasons. A person born on February 29th may be called a 'leapling', a 'leaper', or a 'leap-year baby'. In non-leap years, some leaplings celebrate their birthday on either February 28th or March 1st, while others only observe birthdays on the authentic intercalary date, February 29th.
If this is your big day then 'Happy Birthday'.

March 1st

It is a huge step of faith to admit weakness to gain strength. To go to someone and say, 'Help me please, I can't do this' trusting that the help will be there.

It might be encouragement to keep attempting the seemingly impossible that will be the answer, but not the one wanted or expected. However, through those efforts, under a guiding hand, strength and ability will grow.

It takes more than a mountain of humility in this fast paced, independent, IT led, sound bite world to divest oneself of everything that one's contemporaries perceive as the real me/you and admit that we can't do it alone.

It takes confidence in a loving God to cast off the conscious cloak of external persona; the knowledge, the ability, the leadership, the self-impressionism and say 'just as I am, I come'.

And what Grace is in those outstretched arms waiting to receive us.

What love waits to enfold us, to cover and nurture us.

How wonderful to become an acolyte and know that feeling of surrendering into safety.

March 2nd

I am admitting to real human weakness today, I have a cold. Nothing life threatening but runny nose and runny eyes, prickly throat and maybe a bit of a cough and an overwhelming urge to stay under the duvet. I couldn't though, I had arranged to do a little job for someone and had been in a grump as I made another hot lemon drink and showered. No good grace at all in every move, just a very big 'sorry for myself' grump. Even as I drove off I was consoling myself with a deeply fulfilling grouse about my lot.

Errand done, I rushed home to indulge further in my misery and another hot lemon and then the doorbell rang. The end! The giddy limit! I had half a mind not to answer it except that with a light on it was clear I was at home.

Well, there at the door was someone I hadn't seen in a very long time but who was 'just passing' and wanted to call in. They had tried to phone ahead, I was out but they thought they would try anyway.

I was suddenly recovered and revelled in an impromptu lunch with bright conversation, catching up with lovely company and without a backward glance to 'other me' who had been so miserable earlier. By the time they left, late in the afternoon I had almost forgotten about feeling hard done by and simply felt so happy and blessed.

Thank you for a lovely day Lord.

March 3rd

I might have prayed harder
if I'd known.
If I'd known it would happen
I would have prayed harder.
How does one pray harder?
Do I mean longer?
Do I mean kneeling on a bare floor?
Do I mean fasting and inflicting personal discomfort?
Could I have prayed harder?
STOP
There are no scales by which our prayers are measured.
There is no measure.
There is only the infinite love of God
and the boundless embrace in which he holds us.

March 4th

I had a thank you letter today from the friends who called in unexpectedly.
It was effusive and full of appreciation for the welcome they received, the
lovely lunch, the unfazed way I just seemed to put everything aside to be
with them and make them feel so at home, how well I looked and yes, they
would love to call again next time they are passing.
Surely they weren't referring to the me who had got out of bed that morning
and been such a beastly grump! How many sides there are to a personality,
especially this one and my cold hasn't come to anything much either.

March 5th

I shuffle forward with the crowd in my dirty rags
My worldly possessions in filthy bags and torn
and I see clearer through the mirror of my company
that I have played the biggest trick of deception on myself.
He's a thief, I know it for a fact, what did I steal?
I stole a persona which was less demanding than the one I'd been given.
She's a whore, plays with people's emotions to find love, selfish,
I'm selfish, I keep my stuff close to me where I can see it,
near me where I'd know if anyone helped themselves without my
permission.
Permission, mission, where I can get some soup?
This nightmare is wrong, I'm wrong, I'm not me,
I'm not the me I see.
But maybe through this scrambled kaleidoscope the light
is bending the night hours to hold a mirror to my inside.
To show me what's under the face I present to the world.
Father God let me waken up and know this was a dream.
Father God let me wake up and know how to use the unpalatable truth
Of the damaged me.
Father God thank you for giving me a new beginning with Jesus.

March 6th

Saint Arsenius once said:
'Many times have I spoken and regretted it, but silence I have never
regretted'.
Lord you keep trying to teach me.
How many times do I get this advice in one way or
 another?
Why am I so incapable of just keeping quiet,
of just keeping my opinions to myself,
to be tested before being shared?
I could applaud myself for getting better at it
but it would be conceited because I know
I've a very long way still to go.

March 7th

About holding an opinion as a thought rather than an utterance, perhaps the phrase
'content to live with questions; content to wait for answers'
is appropriate, although that takes some thinking about.
I am conscious of the number of times interviewers chip in with a question before the speaker has finished answering the previous one, cut off from what they wanted to say, and in so doing the interviewer appears impatient and discourteous.
Do I do it? I don't think I need to answer that!

March 8th

Gregory in the 4th century had the sense that, with God there is always more unfolding. That what we can glimpse of The Divine, is always exactly enough and yet never enough.
Ain't that the truth! How often is there an awareness of God's presence to meet a situation head-on after prayerful stillness and how often in our thrill of illumination do we then strive to grasp more, quite inappropriately.
Lord help me to discern the difference between having enough and wanting more, and between having enough and wanting more before I'm ready to digest it.

March 9th

It is pouring down. It isn't just raining it is bucketing down and my spring plants are getting hammered into the earth. The benefit though is that my car is getting washed, hoorah.

It seems a bit shallow to have such thoughts when vast areas of the world would rejoice at this rainfall but I am shallow. I try to be thoughtful but that's when 'I try'. When I let my thoughts 'free stream' I constantly surprise myself at how many of them are not very worthy.

I'm not sure what to do about the thousand and one thoughts that land in my mental 'in-box' like this, uninvited but I remember what dear Rabbi Lionel Blue taught in one of his 'Thought for the Day' slots on Radio 2. We cannot rule thoughts which seem to come in, often so different from what we would perceive as *suitable* so we must look at them for what they are and then offer up an arrow prayer to cover whatever the situation might be.

So, I pray sincerely for the drought stricken places and the various organisations bringing aid to them and am ashamed about seeing my car being washed as an appropriate response to the rain.

March 10th

I do sometimes think how unlovely a lot of the art and iconography of our faith is.

A copious number of adoration paintings have strange odd shaped babies surrounded by cadaverous looking Magi, far from the benevolent grandfatherly figures we might expect; painfully prefiguring the Lord's life and death on the cross, barbarism beyond human comprehension. We praise our risen Lord and simultaneously weep at what he went through for us and the cold dark, heavy interiors in some of our religious buildings make it hard to reconcile our warm and loving Jesus, or the all-embracing forgiveness of our Father God with the inhospitable ambiance.

The reason I've been mulling things over is because of reading about the patterns and representations of Paradise in Islamic art. Although the depiction is not allowed to contain any human form, the harmony between man and nature is celebrated through the work of Muslim gardeners and craftsmen who have taken their inspiration from this union and used it to create, to my eye, very lovely and thoughtful expressions of prayer and praise. They have created places of peace and refreshment laying out gardens, with rills of pure water running in cleansing channels from the four quarters of the garden to a central place, usually a fountain. The quarters are planted with flowers and shrubs, each with a healing or prayerful symbolism, this is a Celestial Garden or Garden of Paradise.

The colours used in Islamic tilework are exquisite and echo the blues of heaven and yellow of sunshine, green for paradise gardens. Peacocks represent the individual person's self and his relationship with the creator, The Almighty. According to tradition the peacock said,

'While people are admiring my beauty, I'm worrying about my hidden faults, whilst they like my colours, I'm worried about my ugly feet'. The lesson is clear, that we should not think too much of ourselves. If the bird is portrayed with its tail outspread, in Sufi mystic iconography, it represents 'the infinite richness of divine beauty, expansive and resplendent'.

Flowers are not admired for their individual beauty so much as for being part of what makes up nature, in itself a symbol of the spirit and generosity of God.

I am not decrying our own Christian masterpieces, merely enjoying seeing how wonderfully another faith uses artistic representation to worship God.

March 11th

I seemed to write a lot yesterday and still I didn't mention the beautiful carpets, rugs and prayer rugs we associate with the Middle East and Islam. Carpets are woven with patterns and colours inspired by the flora and fauna of nature to encourage an expectation of the beauty of celestial Paradise. Usually they are designed to capture the delights of nature in spring and summer, to be enjoyed during the winter months when, in the drier climates of the area, there is less to glory in. Also, the carpets in winter are used to provide warmth and then are generally packed away for the summer to help keep buildings cool.

Apparently, it is not compulsory for Muslims to use a prayer rug, as I had mistakenly thought. There is no absolute rule but having your own prayer rug ensures that there is a clean space on the floor on which to pray and in between times of devotion it is kept folded in a safe place. The rugs are often decorated with images of the Ka'ba and the Prophet's mosque in Medina but may also include arches, flowers and elaborate oil lamps.

I am so pleased to have found these things out and to be able to appreciate some of the beauty and meaning behind the iconography of the arts of Islam.

March 12th

It's snowing!! and it looks like it's sticking. My grandsons are ecstatic. I have enough friends and relatives in the USA and Canada to know that when they see snow they have a different reaction but I just think it looks lovely and special. I'm not going to have to get a snow blower out, or have my drive blocked by a pile of snow as the council plough goes down the road – usually just after I've cleared the drive - as my sister so often bemoans.

But I'm going to get my togs on and have snowball fight, watch out postman!

March 13th

'Search me O God and know my heart.
Test me and know my anxious thoughts,
see if there is any offensive way in me
and lead me in the way everlasting.   Ps.139: 23-24

How long have you got Lord? How big is that little word 'if'?
If there is any offensive way in me! Where to start?
Search me, test me, know my thoughts and worries, there are plenty.
Then the promise and assurance of Gods mercy,
Lead me, I am yours Lord, lead me in the way everlasting.
In your way, walking with you in safety, never alone.

March 14th

Reading back over yesterday's entry I immediately thought of the 23rd
Psalm.
'He makes me to lie down in green pastures, He leads me beside still waters,
He restores my soul'.
When I think of the persecution, exile and betrayal in David's life yet he
could still write with such infinite conviction in the Lord as ultimate
provider, it makes me realise how useless I am and how quickly I become
dispirited and faithless.
Restore my soul to rightness Lord I pray.

March 15th

And what about the opening line of the psalm?
'The Lord is my shepherd'.
David said **my** shepherd. Not just any old shepherd but mine.
The Lord is my what? What is the Lord to me?
This could take a while trying to put into words the indefinable, the otherness yet at the same time the tangible, the illustrative.
An angel suddenly appearing at the door after supplication in need; the loving outreach from an unexpected source. A phone call out of the blue. A real feeling of peace after sitting quietly with Him. My first port of call at the start of the day, the final person I say thank you and goodnight to.
My rock, my everything.
That's what the Lord is to me.

March 16th

I'm going for a walk, it is a glorious day and I'm going to get wrapped up and walk. I'm not going to take any music to listen to either. I think I miss quite a lot with my ear phones in – apart from wandering into the traffic because I don't hear an engine coming up behind me! It has happened, the family would be appalled.
I feel I ought to invite someone who doesn't get out too often, that would be kind. Then I think about how I like to stride out and I wouldn't be able to do so because my friend is hampered with bad feet; how selfish am I? But if I do take the person I'm thinking of she will be pleased and make me feel sainted, I could cope with that. Is that a reason to do something? **NO**.
 Oh Lord why do I make everything such hard work?
 I'm going, on my own.

March 17th

I did walk and it was good but the 23rd psalm came up again and again in my mind.

> 'Though I walk through the valley of the shadow of death…'

This is where I'm attacked, quite often and I feel doom and unrest; for me, for my family members and friends. I then go bigger and more dramatic, the world!! With all the unrest around the globe I feel Armageddon just around the corner. I feel as though I am on the edge of the terrors shown to John in the book of Revelation. The line-up of enemies and powers, frightening visions and symbolic language, beyond my comprehension today, leaves me having to reach for my concordance every time to find the confirmation of Christ's redemption and the vision of 'a new heaven and anew earth'.

Then of course I realise what's happening, what is trying to undermine me and I think back to the words of the psalm,

> 'You are with me; your rod and staff protect me.'

Shepherds of old carried a club to fend off predators and a crook to rescue lame sheep or those fallen by the wayside and Jesus said, 'I am the Good Shepherd'   John 10: 14

Of course, I walk through dark places from time to time, who in life hasn't? But before I get things too far out of perspective I feel the loving crook of Jesus' arm around me, restoring my soul and leading me on.

March 18th

I'm playing catch-up here because I actually didn't write for a couple of days.

Three days ago I was with someone whose cup is always half empty, for whom the world is a miserable place devoid of much joy, light or love….and the thing is that from where I was sitting and what I know of her, she actually has so much!

Her spiritual cup wasn't even half full and yet she spoke with conviction about the love of the Lord and His influence on her life. Really! Where? I felt there was a huge disconnect between her outlook and her in-look but I just didn't want to offer any 'wall-paper' thoughts so I admired her house plants and collection of crystal and talked of general village concerns and after a cup of tea and some time, I left promising to call again before too long.

Two days ago she was heavy on my mind because I really thought I had handled things badly and certainly living by the mantra 'what would Jesus do' I had made a mess of things. I needed to seek God's leading on this and sat for a while at His feet quietly seeking His guidance.

I ended up going round with a posy of spring flowers and was quite open in why I had returned. I said I was sorry if she had felt let down by my visit, that I hadn't just wanted to put a plaster on the hurt without first trying to look at it a bit more so ended up doing nothing. The upshot was that she was kind and generous in her welcome and we prayed together. With a little encouragement, she opened up in such relief it was as though a champagne cork had gone off. I walked home in gratitude to our Father in heaven.

Yesterday I had a lot to do but still wanted to search through what had actually happened over the two preceding days and what I had been taught by it all.

How ready I was to sit in judgement over someone, to make an uneducated assessment of her, her needs and thoughts. How badly I dismissed the clues in her conversation and sought the easy route out. How I never once turned in silent prayer to seek the Lords leading in the situation.

I'm sorry, Father I'm so sorry.

March 19th

Sing unto the Lord a new song!
I have just had my little granddaughter here. We've had all my pans and stainless steel mixing bowls up-ended on the kitchen floor and with two wooden spoons made the best noise ever. It's perhaps as well there are no neighbours but even if there had been, they would surely have felt the joy and immense fun we were having. They might even have been allowed to join in, although it did get a bit proprietorial when my spoon was confiscated so she could do it twice as hard!
Clashing cymbals, oh yes. Music is so subjective.

March 20th

I will never give up hope
or stop praising you.
All day long I will tell of the wonderful things
you do to save your people.
You have done much more than I could possibly know.
I will praise you, Lord God
for your mighty deeds
and your power to save.   Ps.71: 14-16

March 21st

Challenge of the day, at the bottom of a page-a-day note book my dear friend gave me for my birthday;
'The more attached you are to your comfort zone, the less likely you are to realise the extent of your God-given potential'.

That's given me something to think about!

March 22nd

I took time mid-afternoon to have relaxing bath and get ready slowly for a special evening out, instead of flying round at the last minute like I usually do. I thought of it as a part of the whole dinner time, rather like my holiday starting the minute I leave home rather than when I actually reach the destination.
I know yesterday encouraged me to step outside my comfort zone to realise my true God given potential but conversely, stepping into my comfort zone and making time to prepare properly and thoughtfully for this occasion certainly made me feel very much more as though I had made the best of my time and of myself.
I certainly had a lovely evening.

March 23rd

What choice do I have, what choice can I make?
With the world in such turmoil it's a wonder the whole planet isn't being thrown off course.
What voice do I have, what voice can I rise?
With the world in such turmoil one small sound from me isn't going to influence anything.
But I do have a choice and a voice I can use to pray, first and foremost, to my listening Lord
And I do have a choice and voice I can use because I live where I'm free,
to endorse peacemakers, to support those who are brave and go where I wouldn't dare to
in the name of all that is good and true and humane.

March 24th

Because the church calendar is a moveable feast I have endeavoured not to make the days in this journal liturgically based, so that it matters less where and when the pieces are read.

However, it being Lent as I write, I have been brought up short yet again by a familiar verse from Mark 8:34 and I'm not sure it needs to be Lent to challenge me either; but Jesus said 'If any want to become my followers they must deny themselves, take up their cross and follow me'.

I know it isn't just about giving up wine or chocolate – surely not both! for 40 days. I know it isn't just about trying to do something good or kind extra from the norm.

'Take up thy cross' though, surely that means doing something that at least makes me uncomfortable and every time I think along those lines I am drawn back to one place. Why do I find it so hard and difficult to talk about my faith with my own family? I can share, preach and guide to the rest of the world but with my own nearest and dearest I shy away from a direct conversation because I don't want confrontation. I pray for the right opportunity but always chicken out when it presents itself and console myself with the fact that they know what I do and who am and how I live my life and so that will have to do. By example, okay yes?

No, to take up my cross and walk with my Lord this Lent means a bit more commitment from me I think.... I know....I'm sure!

March 25th

Chardonnay, Cherry Ripe, Summer Breeze, Peaches, Apples…what have all these in common? Modern names for baby girls. Invite my opinion on them at your peril.

Here are few others, Mahala, Noah, Hoglah, Milcah, Tirzah. I think they make the first lot sound rather lovely but who are they?

They are the daughters of Zelophehad and were in danger of becoming destitute with no male sibling to take over the family lands on the death of their father. Instead of accepting their lot they took their case to Moses who in turn took it God. God ruled in favour of the women and ruled that the land of the father should go to them. Thus, they were able to enter Cannan with land to call their own and a continuance of their father's name.

The discussion of primogeniture is for another day but the Old Testament can certainly run a fair race in the unusual names stakes.   Book of Numbers 36.

March 26th

Dove

Look at that bird up in that
solitary tree
singing its heart out,
glad to be alive.
It thinks it's in paradise.
Surrounded by squat grey bombed out
blocks of what were dwellings.
Paradise lost.
But that bird is free and can fly away,
can take itself above man's madness.
Paradise regained.

I don't know what sort of a bird you are
but I shall call you
Dove.

I saw a little bird in a tree, on the news last night, during a broadcast from
Syria.

March 27th

'The wind blows where it chooses' and it is certainly doing that today and just like the wind in the book of John 3, I can hear it and yet I don't know where it has come from or where it is going. The weather forecast certainly got it wrong.

I'm not Nicodemus though. I don't need to question Jesus about using the wind as a metaphor of movement for the Holy Spirit.

No, I can't see it, or feel it, or hear it, or taste it on any sensory level, the Holy Spirit that is. But I can see the effects in the lives of people, I can see the results of prayer in repair and regrowth of relationships. I see and feel the tide of movement from intractable to possible in situations beyond mere human endeavour.

The fruits of the Spirit are living proof of the intangible wind.

Loving Lord blow though me and make me more productive in your Kingdom here on earth.

March 28th

How do you define success?

Dr Kathleen Wiggins posed this question to the congregation at Siesta Key Chapel, Florida.

As ever her preaching was inspirational and exacting and encouraging and certainly spirit filled. We were led through the various interpretations of 'success' from commercial and secular to biblically sound and something to be striven for.

Then came the whammy.

What would you have said about you at your funeral?......................

How do I define 'success' in my life? How would I like it to be defined at my funeral?

March 29th

St Augustine wrote of reading the Bible as 'love letters from home'.
How can four short words convey so much? It certainly changes my
receptivity and involvement, commitment and belonging.

March 30th

ACTS
Adoration
Confession
Thanksgiving
Supplication
A little model with enormous potential to transform a personal prayer life.
It just needs a commitment to practice.
Our Jewish friends meet with God three times a day (Ps 55:17) and in Islam
prayer is prescribed five times a day. I know we Christians think that God
will love us whatever we can give him but a little more effort wouldn't go
amiss I'm sure. This is a plan that is too simple to be ignored.

March 31st

Life is bursting out all over the place. Not quite June bursting out all over just yet but bursting out there is, everywhere. The flowers and blossom are gorgeous, it's a pleasure to walk to the shops or cycle to the gym. It's a joy to drive across the countryside to our daughter's cottage or through the lanes to get our grandsons from school.

Thank you for the ability to say thank you, for the ability to notice, for the lack of pain, mental or physical.

Lord help me to remember and treasure this surfeit of loveliness against the times of angst and unrest which from time to time descend and block my appreciation.

April 1st

Here's my lightbulb moment from yesterday whilst reading an article on developing one's faith, some of which challenged me to argue – what's new there?

My question arising is this, why are we always trying to understand and interpret God's message? We're not that bright, we're not that clever, we're not that omnipotent.

I know we pray for discernment and understanding but just sometimes I feel as though we over analyse and lose sight of the command in Cor.2:10

'But it was to us that God made known his secret by means of his spirit. The spirit searches everything, even the hidden depths of God's purposes'.

'The hidden depths of Gods purposes.'

Instead of exhausting myself in research and exegesis and reading and 'doing', Lord let me just be with you and hear what you want me to hear. Reveal to me, in measure of my understanding, the power of your message and thank you for showing me the damage I can do by over working things.

April 2nd

Thinking about over-working things, I know I don't always do somethings because of fear of failure, and why is fear there? Because I have over-thought a situation. Then when it, whatever, happens I am constantly relieved that things were not as bad as I had feared.

'Fear not' appears 366 times in the bible – once for every day of the year, including leap year and so 'fearing' means we are disobeying God's will for us. Fear NOT.

Fear of what could happen, might happen, the what ifs and how, why and when, cripples us from stepping out in faith. It stops us, it blocks God's power. Where is that influence coming from Not from the Lord that's for sure. 2 Timothy 1:7 exhorts us 'to fan into flame not fear. God has not given a spirit of fear'.

In feeling fear or threat we immediately make a barrier of self-protection around us and that in turn blocks the love and generosity of our Lord.

What could be worse than facing being fed to the lions? That was fear.

Lord help me to feel fear only in proportion to the situation, knowing that I am never alone or apart from you.

April 3rd

Father for my friends I thank you.
Wrap them in my shawl of appreciation woven from days and months and years of knowing.
Made from threads of laughter and fun, of crying and holding, of talking and sitting in silence.
Stitched with trust and complete freedom to be ourselves as individuals, warts and all.
This shawl is seamless there are no joins because we are one, this shawl has no earthly measure because it reaches round us all, the only binding is you Lord.
Nurturing us as we nurture each other, protecting as we protect each other.
I like to think that one day in a beautiful garden we will spread this shawl on the heavenly ground and have a wonderful celebration of our togetherness with a delicious picnic.
Oh, and thank you Lord that my friends all love food.

April 4th

Talking of food, I have started to explore a wonderful cook book called 'Jerusalem' written by Yotam Ottolenghi along with his friend Sami Tamimi. The book celebrates the food of the two friends home city, one a Jew and the other a Muslim, they have compiled a fusion of cross cultural deliciousness.
It was a Christmas present from my daughter who knows I enjoy exploring new recipes. The amazing thing is how easily we can now get a hold of all the exotic spices and seasonings that enable us to share in the cuisines of the world. Maybe we can begin to know and understand folks of diverse cultures over a meal table and grow trust from the herb garden, rather than antagonism out of unknowing.

April 5th

And another thing.
A very senior churchman friend of ours has a magnet on his fridge which states that 'If there isn't chocolate in heaven I'm not going', Could I please add to that Lobster? Expensive, ridiculous, an extremely special treat, yes. Would I miss it in heaven, I shouldn't think so with all the other good things on offer but just thought I'd mention it.

April 6th

I don't think I'm really dumb but sometimes, when I have had to have something on the computer explained for the 10th time, I begin to wonder. I hear every word, I think I'm taking it in and making the right neural connections to remember but then poooof! I try to repeat the exercise alone and get into the same fix as before. No one is harder on me than I am on myself and my frustration so often boils over on to the next moving thing walking by, usually my husband, the one who has so patiently tried to help me in the first place.
It happens too often and I am aware that my reaction is against the realisation that I'm probably not as receptive as I once was to new technologies because I'm not as young as I once was. There I've said it! There's nothing wrong with me, praise the Lord and I am fit, well and active but one or two things must be acknowledged and until I can have some anti-aging nanospheres inserted into my frontal lobe, where the short term or working memory happens, then I'm stuck.
Lord grant me graceful acceptance of the things I can't change.

April 7th

It's a conundrum morning.   Matt 18:2-4 exhorts me to have the faith of a child. I know that doesn't mean blind trust that could easily lead me astray but rather to be humble and without guile.

 I am not naturally a suspicious person, though neither do I walk through life clothed in gullibility.

Then in 1 Thess. 5:21 I'm told 'Put all things to the test: keep what is good and avoid every kind of evil'.

To have sufficient discernment to know what is 'good, to keep' takes maturity which sometimes has been achieved through less guileless and less humble experiences and to 'avoid every kind of evil' calls for awareness, suspicion, warning antennae.

Spiritual growth and maturity certainly has nothing to do with birthdays.

April 8th

In my work as a Spiritual Director I am sometimes asked to take part in weeks of guided prayer for churches and individuals wanting to experience deeper awareness of their time with the Lord. Here the discussion from yesterday about child like faith is very pertinent because of one's approach to prayer.

Many tomes have been written on the 'how to' of establishing a solid prayer life but my first position has to be that we approach this time we have set aside as a holy space. Then, that we come in wonder and awe before God, the wonder and awe that is truly transformative and deeply meditative.

Of course, one should teach a child to pray and to learn to respect their time with Jesus as very special and then there will hopefully come a time when they will want more than a milk diet.   Heb.5: 13

April 9th

'But if any of you lacks wisdom, he should pray to God who will give it to him: because God gives generously and graciously to all. But, when you pray, you must believe and not doubt at all. Whoever doubts is like a wave on the sea that is driven and blown about by the wind. A person like that, unable to make his mind up, and undecided in all he does, must not think that he will receive anything from the Lord'.   James 1: 5-8

April 10th

All this talk of child-like things made me think of milk so I decided to make one of Peter's favourite desserts, a proper, baked rice pudding. His mother made the best ones in her Rayburn (like an Aga) and cooked long and slow they were wonderful, I usually resort to a tin I'm afraid.

I waited, oven gloves poised to present the sweet, golden delight to my expectant spouse.

My offering was solid, overcooked and pathetic, sliced up it would have made good building blocks.

Note to self – either practice or stick to buying tins.

April 11th

I'm so excited, we are looking after a dog for the week-end. We have missed Tilly our old black lab but we really don't want to take on another one now with a little more freedom to enjoy. That sounds selfish but we enjoy travelling when we can, either with the caravan or further afield and, also to visit friends around the country, so it wouldn't be fair to keep putting a dog into kennels.

Anyway, we enjoy being able to share the dogs belonging to our daughter and various friends so actually we have the best of both worlds. Like grandchildren they come, you spoil them and then they go home.

April 12th

What good does laughter do?

It is such a tonic, such a boost, such an uninhibited sharing with someone, a bonding moment whether with a long-term friend, partner or child.

The poor old Philosopher in Ecclesiastes says in desperation that he decided to enjoy himself and find happiness but found it was useless and that laughter was foolish. He is a poor specimen and proof that someone who appears to have everything materially can still be an unhappy wreck.

Thank God for laughter. I've said it before and I'll say it again.

April 13th

I have just read a wonderful book **Gilead** *by Marilynne Robinson.*
John Ames says to his son Calvin, during a conversation trying to get into the mind of God, rather a challenge but anyway, 'Each if us is an actor on stage and God is the audience'. Now the continuing conversation is for the story but that comment is surely one to ponder on.
If I'm an actor I don't think I'm being myself, I'm playing a part. I do it though, we all do. Days when I'd rather be at home alone, pleasing myself, but have to be at a meeting or visiting someone instead, but I put on an act of genial compliance with the situation, sometimes inwardly grudgingly.
However, I don't think that I could keep putting on an act for very long, the mask would soon slip and I would be exposed for the fraud I am. I believe that God, seeing me all the time, knows me better than I know myself and while I try always to please him I know I fall far short of the mark every day. I don't think of him as a theatre critic, if he was he would have walked out long ago demanding his money back.
I hide behind no theatricals with the Lord.

April 14th

Hospital Chaplaincy Day.

There is so much hurt in this place today,
sad not glad faces give away
the pain and heartache of loving
too much.
Fragile life, damaged, frightened,
frail but brave
for the sake of the rest.
How many ways to say good bye
but don't go just yet.
I know you're tired, you've had enough
and we can't manage the strain
much longer.
The window to your stillness is opening
slowly as the one on this world closes.
Yet this is a place of contrasts
as an exuberant child
clutching a balloon barrels down the landing
to meet very soon his new baby sister.
One comes in and one goes out
and heaven will supply to each,
nascent hope for the future
and peace for a soul released.

April 15th

It was a hard day at the hospital yesterday, or perhaps I was just feeling things more than usual, and so it was a joy to see that little one with his balloon rushing headlong into the maternity ward and a new family member. Lord be with all young families working to raise children, the next generation, in such a climate of change and uncertainty and bless and strengthen those whose job it is to support and care for them through the valuable and vulnerable early years.

April 16th

'His preaching will turn the hearts of children to their fathers.'   Malachi 4:4
God wants families to be units working together, safe in his love and safe under the banner of his rule. I hope this rightness will be restored in heaven because here on earth matters of faith and religion seem to cause more division and friction than anything else.

April 17th

Headline in the financial paper this morning:
                    'The power lies in the profit'
May I suggest:
                    'The power lies in the Prophet'

April 18th

Talking of prophets, preaching in the northern kingdom of Israel in 721 BC, Hosea was concerned at the faithless idolatry of the people. He reminds them, after admonishing them, about the Lord's goodness and mercy; in turning back to God and remaining faithful Hosea tells them what the Lord promised:
'I will bring the people back to me, I will love them with all my heart and be no longer angry with them. They will blossom like flowers, firmly rooted like the trees of Lebanon. They will be alive with new growth, they will be fragrant, they will live under my protection…The people of Israel will have nothing more to do with idols, I will answer their prayers and take care of them; like an evergreen tree I will shelter them; I am the source of all their blessings'.   Ho. 14: 4-8

What a beautiful vision of immeasurable love. …for us all.

April 19th

Lunch with girlfriends today and I feel like I've been to a health spa. Why don't we do it more often? Why do we always seem too busy? Busy doing what!
Oh, the diary looks full and the calendar is covered in entries, mine in blue, Peter's in purple so we can show anyone who cares to look that we really are very busy people. How much of it is crucial? How much of it is important? How much of it is even necessary? More fundamentally, how much is to make me feel needed or indispensable? Not everything but there's room for change.
'Let's do it again before too long', we agreed as we went our separate ways, and we will, I'm going to make sure of it.

April 20th

Perhaps a day at a spa was a step too far when I went on line to research it. It just seemed like a great idea for me and my pals after yesterday's lunch. The treatments on offer, the masks and wraps, came with promises of such rejuvenation that I would be frightened I wouldn't recognise the new me or the others. The thalassotherapy sounded like 'the lass on therapy' so I was left in a quandary as to what it entailed and the 'deep electronic sub-dermal manipulation' sounded like something from a Bond film and not altogether pleasurable. Beside each entry on the e-page was the cost…………..
…………….. Do you know what? We can have champagne with our next lunch, as much fun and laughter as before, every month for a year for that amount.
Get your diaries out girls.

April 21st

The collect for today reads:
> God, our judge and saviour
> teach us to be open to your truth
> and to trust in your love that we may
> live each day with confidence in the salvation
> which is given through Jesus Christ our Lord.
> Amen.

I put it in the first person, claim it and make it personal, what more does this day need?

April 22nd

'God my Judge and Saviour'.
The first line of yesterday's collect, a real juxtaposition of images and quite a challenge to contemplate.
Firstly 'God my Judge', the stern, slightly cross, bearded man of the Old Testament. OK a simplistic and childish evocation but I think probably one with which many folks reared in Sunday schools in the 50's would identify.
Then, 'and Saviour'
Next an image of our Saviour, Jesus, shepherd, suffering children to climb on his knee and be loved, be kept safe.
These two seemingly incompatible images, when thought about in simple human terms, are safe in their separateness. Now I must close my eyes and see the one morph into the other, like the effects so available to us now through computer generated imaging.
What am I left with?
Not pictures but a feeling, a knowledge, a conviction, an overwhelming emotion of security and safety and the continuing promise that, trusting in that love I may live each day with confidence in the salvation which is given through Jesus Christ our Lord.

April 23rd

It's quite early but I've been awake a while thinking. Sometimes, when I have chewed over a meditation that has been tough but ultimately rewarding, I feel I need to give myself permission to be free of philosophising for a day.

So today will be one where I will pray when I'm out and about and feel like saying a prayer. It might be about a tree or a dog, a piece of bad parking or a car passing me by with the music rocking it on its axles. I will not read any set text supporting my daily walk with God but will wait on Him to instruct me through what I see on the side of vans or hoardings, maybe there will be something, maybe nothing particular. Whatever comes my way I am open, unfettered and excited.

April 24th

The strange thing about my plans for yesterday was that they were thrown into turmoil very early on. Firstly, not long after breakfast it rained, heavily, thus scuppering my plan for walking to the shops. Then a phone call from someone needing prayer support and a shoulder to cry on found me off down the motorway with some haste, praying through traffic and spray from lorries to get to my friend as quickly as possible. Her problems are ongoing but we both felt the presence of the Lord during our time together and a feeling of peace that we had restored some faithful equilibrium into her situation. When I got home I had another time of prayer for her and reached for my bible.

So much for a day of freewheeling!

April 25th

Still keep thinking 'God my Judge and Saviour'.

Perhaps my initial interpretation was just that, initial, and that deeper pondering, rather like with a lectio divina, has brought new understanding to me.

If someone is capable of saving me, of being my saviour, with all the promise meant by that, not just earthly but eternally; surely then that person is also more than qualified to judge me and show me the errors of my ways that I might be worthy of saving.

I for my part must be willing to be under such holy scrutiny and be ready to be discovered falling far short. I must be ready and willing to be searched for my own good, my own growth and all with the faith that he who wants this from me wants nothing in return other than my love and faithfulness. Wow!

April 26th

I'm an amateur gardener and I know how long things take to grow, to slowly turn from a small cutting or seedling in to something fully mature. Why then do I expect my spiritual growth to be fast? Can I not see that I would be like a plant that has bolted, weak and floppy and of very little use, too sickly to survive?

Lord grant me vision to see and appreciate what you are doing with me.

Lord grant me patience to accept your growing process.

April 27th

The Lord said:
'I am sending you grain, new wine, and olive oil, enough to satisfy you.'

Joel 2: 19

Here are seasons of growth to contemplate:

Grain. An annual harvest from seed, something very tangible in its growth, being and purpose.

Wine. Grape seed to productive vine in 10 years. Much tending and patient nurturing to a satisfactory product.

Olive Oil. Pip to oil thirty five to forty years. Well into another generation, another whole spectrum of patient tending.

We or rather I, need to discern the season I am in and let the Lord tend and nurture me according to his plan, not mine.

April 28th

'At God's command, amazing things happen, wonderful things that we can't understand.'

Job 37: 5

The rest of this chapter is in complete praise to the power of God but this one verse is short enough and simple enough and true enough for a 'sound bite' of affirmation.

April 29th

Last evening I had one of my regular Skypes with my sister in Canada, a glass of wine for me, pre-dinner, and a cup of coffee for her after her lunch. We had a great catch up, good old sister to sister beef about nothing in particular, a bit of reminiscing about things our mother used to say and do, frustrations with people in general, we also acknowledged the advances in technology which have made our communicating so much easier and immediate.

When my children were small I was living in Germany and having to exist on a short, expensive phone call fortnightly back to home, that and having to wait for photographs - also expensive - to come back from the developer before I could update Ma and Pa on their grandchildren. How the grannies would have adored being able to see and talk to their little people and us.

I know I grumble about much computerised interference now deemed necessary to everyday life, but somethings really are wonderful and I am grateful for them.

April 30th

'Shine Jesus Shine' what a super modern hymn, song, whatever we must call them now.

The tune is wonderfully lyrical and builds with the words into a poem of praise set to music. Shine, blaze, fill, what words of empowering encouragement to me.

Ironically, I sing it when I really need to hang on, when I'm really not feeling the shine, blaze or surfeit of Godliness.

'Forth in thy name oh Lord I go, my daily labour to pursue,
Thee only thee resolved to know, in all I think and speak and do'.
Another good standby I think.

May 1st

It is raining this morning, actually, it's tipping down, and I have just driven home from town behind someone in need of either more driving lessons or having their licence taken off them. Or so I thought. The awful thing was they were prominently displaying a rainbow 'fish' sticker on the back of their car, proclaiming their faith.

So, I felt that I should be more charitable knowing it was a fellow Christian. WHY!

Going over cautiously, then speeding up, indicating a change of direction, not once but several times, when there was nowhere to turn, oh and with no lights on. No, my irritation was justified.

But there was that rainbow fish being ushered into view every other second by my wiper blades.

Were they lost? Were they on new territory? Was there a fractious child in the car? Was the driver unwell?

I simmered down and prayed, mainly to thank God for the visual reminder of his ever-present love.

The shocking thing is that without the fish sticker I would have remained in a self-righteous grump all the way home.

May 2nd

To my Grieving Friend

I have no words
My sigh is my prayer
In my cupped hands
I lift you
Beyond sight
Beyond knowing
Towards the centre
of our faith
The unseen
The ever compassionate
The ever loving
and holding
Jesus.

May 3rd

'Life is short', 'Seize the day', 'You never know what's around the corner'.
Yesterday those platitudes were all that we kept repeating, suddenly the
portents of doom were very real and yet totally ineffective in beginning to
explain or ease our deep shock at the loss of our friend, so suddenly, so
undeservedly, when is it deserved I know, but…so very unjustly.
So many questions for God but no answers and I'm not ready to just lie
back and try to claim his peace, I need to be angry. Very angry, for a
beautiful, loving, faithful family heartbroken and in shock.

May 4th

I went to church, to a lunchtime Eucharist. Not a church I've ever been to in the city before but one whose service banner seemed to float right out at ME.
Thank God for Jesus. Thank God for my faith.
I'm still devastatingly sad but I have climbed back into the arms of the company of the saints and angels where answers aren't needed, just an overwhelming feeling that with this amount of holy support we will all pull through.

May 5th

Why am I surprised that my reading for today is so perfect?
'For we know that if the earthly tent we live in is destroyed we have a building from God, a house not made with hands but eternal, in the heavens.'

2 Cor.5: 1

May 6th

We have had the afternoon watching our grandson playing cricket in his school team. It was a great afternoon of cheering and commiserating, of shouting and laughter and sharing. We needed it, we needed to be reminded that life is huge and precious; that the scales of emotions should be levelled off for good to eventually outweigh pain.

A team of dirty, triumphant, noisy eleven year olds wolfing down a post-match tea of sausage and chips is a most wholesome and affirming sight. Thank you, Lord.

May 7th

It's been a 'good washing day'. High clouds, a fair breeze and sweet late spring air with no trace of damp wintery left-overs. Sad, old fashioned maybe that I still get pleasure from pegging the washing out and bringing it in dry, smelling of the wind. I remember when, in our first little flat, there was just the back balcony by the rubbish chute for me to stand a clothes rack. Usually it had to be brought in to be aired off but even that little outside time made such a difference, or at least I thought so.

In this country so many more folk live in houses than in continental Europe but figures suggest that fewer people than ever have a washing line of one sort or another. What a sad waste of God's resources.

May 8th

I am in a group looking at ways to meet peoples' spiritual needs, within the wider diocese and at a more local level. Many words are used to talk about matters of faith but what are we actually meaning by them? We all know, or think we know what 'spirituality' means yet everyone will have his or her own unique reaction to the word and experience.

It was this frustration which led Rudolph Otto (German Lutheran Theologian 1869-1937) to write his treatise 'The Idea of the Holy'. A work where he attempts to address the 'Idea of the divine and its relation to the rational' and to explore the non-rational elements of religion. We must beware of the semantics here, we are thinking about 'non-rational', not. 'irrational'.

I sometimes wonder about the language of our Christian faith eighty years on, in this secular age and how sensitive we are when talking about it with people of other or no belief.

May 9th

Dear Heavenly Father,
A door is no more when it is open.
A door only works when it is closed.
May my door be open
to bless comings and goings
and may people know that
even when shut it isn't closed.
A heart is alive when it is beating
but can still be open or closed
to life around it.
May my heart be open to
God's spirit leading me through
the warp and weft
of the life I live.   Amen

May10th

So much happens in a day. So many chance meetings and conversations, so many seemingly innocent threads which, later it becomes apparent, were a part of something bigger. The secular world calls these things coincidence or luck but for people of faith we know there is a greater working-out going on. It isn't always easy to encourage a group to look beyond the everyday, here and now, but a quiet encouragement to a different way of looking at things is often an opportunity for a gentle affirmation of our faith.
The post script to this is that I need to remind myself to look for the hand of God in the coincidences.

May 11th

Today we walked to church without coats. It was so warm, hot in fact, that we came home and decided to BBQ our lunch. We sat in our little garden under the ornamental cherry tree, still clinging onto its blossom and read the paper and felt euphorically grateful and happy. No big announcements or revelations of world shattering importance, just a simple, lovely Sunday.

May 12th

I'm sitting at my desk with the windows open and thinking about yesterday's sermon.
Do I define myself by who I am, what I do, how other people perceive me, where I'm going?
Where am I going? Who am I? What do I do and for whom?
I am not the person I was when I was when I was working. Then I had a job spec and title to define me. I'm not the person I was when the children were still at home and I was Jo's mum, Jeni's mum or Richard's mum.
What I am, I hope, is a jobbing member of the community in which we now live. A place where we have been accepted, not for who we were or what we had, but for who we are now, loved and appreciated for what we have brought with us in the way of willingness to join in and serve where needed.
We are also open to receive the generous warmth of our new friends and neighbours as a gift from the Holy Spirit, confirming the rightness of who we are and where we are right now.

May 13th

How often have I had someone say to me 'I can't pray, I don't know how to pray'. Why do so many faithful souls still think there is some ritualistic magic to praying?

I never try to give them an answer there and then but try to find out a little more about why thy say what they do and very often they end up finding some answers for themselves.

'I guess I don't make time', 'I'm just too busy', 'Our house is so noisy'.

I used the quotation from Dr Martin Israel on the cover of my last book, he wrote,

'God is eternally present, it is we, who are seldom at home to receive him'.

Just standing and acknowledging our Father God is a start. No organ voluntary or clashing cymbals needed. There was a little book doing the rounds of our church youth group many years ago called 'Hello God, it's Gemma here'. That's a prayer.

May 14th

How to help someone pray?
The Rule of the Sisters of the Love of God includes a chapter entitled Silence in Prayer and it begins:

> 'Silence shall be regarded as one of the chief privileges of the Community, for it prepares the way for the union of the soul with the will of God and is an offering of perpetual reverence to his majesty.'

Just like Dr Israel's words, the emphasis here is on coming with honest openness and willingness to meet God. This is not about a hurried arrow prayer in an immediate situation but prayer to deepen ones relationship with the Father. The Sisters of the Love of God is a contemplative order whose function and purpose is prayer and we might think that it would be easy to be good at prayer if we were removed from the world. However, the Sisterhood is very much in touch and aware of what besets the rest of humanity and offers everything before God in prayer with conscientious affection from peeling vegetables to feed their guests, to the observation of the five daily offices. As it is written, all undertaken 'as an offering of perpetual devotion'.

May 15th

Before I leave the subject I think one more of Martin Israel's thoughts is worth dwelling on, he writes in his prologue to 'Precarious Living'

'Every experience in life is a key to deeper understanding providing we have the wisdom to be still and ask the right questions.'

What questions should I be asking?

May 16th

Loving Lord
I know that in my vulnerability
I grow closer to you.
I know that in my sadness I lean
more heavily on you.
I know that in my bewilderment
I let you take the reins and
the burdens which I can
no longer lift, even
in prayer, are eased.
So Lord by your grace
alone I call myself your child and ask
you to meet me at my point
of need today. Help me to hear,
to discern and know
                your will for me.   Amen

May 17th

It's the middle of the night again, 3 am and I am wide awake. It is strange that I don't feel more frustrated about it but in fact I rather like this deep, time of quiet where a blanket of silence, usually wrapped around me in sleep, is here for me to appreciate. It feels like I can own a piece of the night, just for me, and it feels like a privilege. It is certainly a special opportunity to sit with God. Not to be talking, praying or filling him in on my thoughts and opinions but just to sit with him.

What was it the Sisters of the Love of God have written in their Rule?

'Silence shall be regarded as one of the privileges of the community' and I can appreciate why in many houses of prayer the day begins even before dawn with a time of collective silence, strengthening and cementing, reawakening appreciation in the totality of God's love for us.

May 18th

I'm not tired. I think I should be?

After an hour and a half of wakefulness I ought to be but I feel very refreshed. It might catch up with me later this afternoon but this morning I feel like I'm still wrapped in a duvet of devotion and ready to take on the day. I could let my cynicism begin to undermine this feeling of well-being but in recognising it I will try to ignore it and instead remember and treasure the very lovely, very gracious time I was given, alone with my Lord.

May 19th

Children's laughter.
Is there a more infectious sound?   I seem to have been surrounded by it today. Firstly, it was obviously play time when I walked to the village and so the joyous noise from the school rang out across the duck pond as I passed by, then, later on, much laughter and chatter as the various little groups came past my study window on their way home. It was all topped off with a Skype to our grandchildren before they went to bed and they kept collapsing with mirth at a funny incident they were trying to share with us. We all ended up breathlessly silly, and it was great.
Spontaneous bursts of an emotion that only we human beings have and which children seem to have in abundance. What a pity it gets some of the edges knocked off as life takes over.

May 20th

'What we say and what we do need to be equal'
This was a small phrase in an interview with Tadashi Yanai - Founder of Uniqlo, the fourth biggest clothing retail clothing company in the world, about the global lack of respect for quality and the manpower associated with its production.
'What we say and what we do need to be equal'
That phrase leapt out at me, not because I know about the man or his product but because it seemed to be challenging me. Me. I who profess to be a Christian.
Are what I say and what do equal?

May 21st

I've been shopping with a dear friend today. She hasn't been very well and this trip out was really a test of her stamina as well as a change of scene. Well, the stamina wasn't over-taxed.

We went for coffee when we got to town, that was a leisurely hour and half catching up on all the family news, and between us that's quite a lot. Also, a general reprise of the goings on in our lives since we last met properly…...on our own I mean.

A little wander and window shop through the precinct led us to Carluccio's where our table was booked for a celebratory 'recovery' lunch and another long sit down. What did we talk about? I don't know but we are never stuck, we have so many things in common, books, recipes, mutual friends, old colleagues, gardening.

Eventually we left the restaurant and walked slowly back through the arcade, popping into a couple of places to try on some shoes in one and a sweater in another but bought neither in the event.

Thought about a cup of tea before we parted but decided we really didn't need it so went our separate ways after huge hugs and 'I love yous'.

No shopping but a great deal of genuine trust, love and friendship.

I wouldn't have been able to buy those anyway.

May 22nd

The Lord bless you and keep you.
The Lord make his face to sine upon you and be gracious unto you.
The Lord turn his face towards you and give you peace.

Numbers 24-26

My prayer last night for my friend.

May 23rd

May is a lovely month and it is usually the month I go to visit my sister in Canada but I'm not going this year because she is coming over in September. I thought I would feel a bit sad, it is something I really look forward to and enjoy but because the weather has been so wonderful I am appreciating being here in England. The hawthorn hedge opposite our house is so newly green, it is almost shouting 'look at me' and there is so much going on in the garden and the allotment that I wonder how I could ever bear to leave it for 10 days. Then I feel sad at not seeing my sister for another few months so I make a cup of coffee, Skype her, see and hear her and again be so thankful for this amazing technology.

May 24th

The realisation that The Church, of whatever denomination, is so often seen to be a long way from the Kingdom is shocking. We pray daily in The Lord's Prayer 'Your Kingdom come' but what do we mean, what do we think, do we think at all?
God's Kingdom of justice, love and peace seems a long way off when I listen to arguments for and against life's debates. They need to take place, there must be a forum for issues to be examined, opinions heard and theologies analysed in the light of where we are today. I know all this and yet sometimes all I see is a table around which is gathered a body of individuals, each with their own agenda, each with their own soap box, each with their own ego and precious little acknowledgement of genuine commitment. Another Synod, another Council of Churches, another confirmation that the gulf between us as Christians is as wide as the gulf between us and any other faith.
There, I've said it!

May 25th

'For the Kingdom, the power and the glory are yours'
There's that word again, Kingdom. So here I am, just me. I can't take on the world, or even the ruling bodies of the Christian Church in England. What I can try to do is be the best citizen possible under the rule of my king, King Jesus. Also I can claim those promises, that the power and the glory which he possesses are mine too, through remaining faithful and believing in the supreme grace on offer to me. And that probably means being more generous to those on church councils and administrative bodies who do *sincerely* believe they are trying to build the Kingdom of God here on earth.

May 26th

It's hot, summer is here. I love it, the windows are all open and the air feels good and I'm in a tee shirt.
I remember, according to my mother's aphorism 'ne're casting a clout 'til May is out', that all pretence at lightening up one's clothing was a actually a portent of doom. An invitation to all manner of ill and chill to attack a hitherto unprepared, muffled up body. She could never grasp my logic, that a week either way on the calendar was not going to make a difference to my immunity. That whether May being May blossom or May the month, me leaving off a few pieces of clothing would not consign me to the mercies of sick-bay.
Now our homes are a lovely temperature all year round, all the areas of our homes are more evenly managed according to personal comfort and I'll wager that my mother would be the first to relish not being wrapped up like some Russian babushka for the winter. Of course, she probably wasn't as old fashioned as I remember, there's a surprise, but one's teenage memories are rather prone to bias. Come to that I wonder how many of my long-term memories are flawed.

May 27th

One memory that certainly isn't flawed is the one about the Billy Graham Crusade in Manchester at Old Trafford. The 'old' Old Trafford, in June 1961. I recently found a slip of paper in my grandmother's little old King James Bible, written by me around that time when I was 13 years old.

Lord my senses jangle as
I try to untangle the puzzle
of faith.
You knocked at the door to my heart and I flew
into your arms.
You chose me, by your grace and I'm saved not
by my charms or my own works
the pace of which is unreliable.
You chose me but I could have said no.
Free-will could have meant me to go
through the rest of my life without you.
Dead.

That's one memory which as clear as the day and which I treasure.

May 28th

'The word of God is living and active.
It judges the thoughts and intentions of the heart.
All is open and laid bare before the eyes of him whom
to whom we must give account.
We confess our sines in penitence and faith.'

Hebrews 4: 12

There is truth and challenge in every word of this verse.

May 29th

This was one of the first verses I committed to memory after that night at Old Trafford and no I don't know why, apart from the insistence of our 'crusade mentors' that we should learn a verse-a-day out of a perforated book.

I thought at the time that my sincerity to become a good, saved Christian was measure by the number of tear-out tokens I collected and thanks to a good memory some have remained with me.

This one has also grown with me across the years and still today takes me to places within myself that I'm glad no-one else knows about…except God himself, Judge of all.

It is because his word is living and active that I can still explore, learn and know more of his wondrous gifts, that even fifty six years on from the Billy Graham Crusade I am still drawn to confess my sins in 'penitence and faith' knowing I am forgiven, totally and without measure of how many verses I can or can't remember.

May 30th

Someone asked me the other day why I never discussed the political hot-potatoes of the day in my **Coffee Pot Journal**. Admittedly here were a few issues which crept in but now, with hindsight, I am glad that it didn't become an historically motivated collection and here's why, and, why I have deliberately attempted to put in even fewer into **Another Pot of Coffee**. The first book went into five editions across eight years and travelled to the USA and Canada as well as Australia and New Zealand.

It was only ever intended to be a modest but gently thought provoking way of sharing the good news of my faith with a few chums, pals, friends of faith or non. So, firstly I didn't need to regurgitate the news and now it would seem, that for a lot of people around the world who have come to know and love the book, comments of a political nature would have been less relevant anyway.

My rational seems weak now I have committed it to print but I think I'll stick with it.

May 31st

How to spell serendipitous?
I was reading through some notes recommended to me by a friend in Chicago last night, sermons by a writer called Professor Alan Jacobs who wrote:
'If I can bring to an issue heat, but no light, it is probably best that I remain silent.'
I was thinking about it terms of my response yesterday initially but goodness me, I then looked again at the enormity of the statement.
'If I can bring to an issue heat, but no light, it is probably best that I remain silent.'
Note to self – commit that one to memory!

June 1st

O Happy Day! a friend has been given the all clear after months of bruising treatment, prayers have been answered and we can dance with joy and gratefulness.
Forgotten are the times of desolation when we thought our prayers were not being heeded, when we became sad and frightened about our seemingly futile intercessions of her behalf. What did we expect, a magic wand from the clouds to somehow prove God was listening! How pathetic we are at letting ourselves be tossed around on the tides of human emotions whilst going through the motions of faithful obedience.
Now as I rejoice with my friend, I feel more aware of the pain of the families we got to know who are still walking the road of treatment and for some of whom, there will be a less celebratory outcome.

June 2nd

Dog sitting day. An excuse to ignore non-essentials and go to the country park for the morning. I should offer to do this more often I think, since I seem to need a valid excuse to take time out.
I had forgotten how bad wet dog and pond weed can smell though!

June 3rd

'Vanity is by its very nature selfish'. I heard this statement on the radio as I closed the car door and rather like part of an overheard conversation on the bus, it left me wondering. I know I can go back to 'listen again' and hear the whole piece and maybe I will but in the meantime, I have been pondering on that phrase on and off all day.
'Vanity **is** by its very nature selfish.' It's true because surely the essence of vanity is that it can only exist by dint of the effect on self or another person…. I do this that they will notice…. I do this to make me look better, smell nicer, sound more accomplished.
However, neither vanity nor selfishness are necessarily negative behaviours but need to be recognised and managed appropriately for the good of self or others.

June 4th

I decided to look up what the other deadly sins were and found that Vanity wasn't one of them though it could come under Pride. There are of course Greed, Lust, Envy, Gluttony, Anger and Sloth.
In dissembling semantics, couldn't Greed and Gluttony be conflated or perhaps Envy and Lust be merged?
Perhaps I just don't want to walk up the slopes of Mount Purgatory with Dante.

June 5th

In all the introspection about Capital Vices, Cardinal Sins, behaviours and habits, perhaps the overriding thing to remember is that as Christians we walk IN victory not Towards it. We journey with JOY.

'You will make known to me the path of life, you will fill me with joy in your presence.'
Ps 16: 11

June 6th

Joy came up again in this morning's reading, perhaps there's a message here!
'The fruit of the spirit is joy.'

Gal. 5: 22

Joy is a proactive emotion though because we have to work with the Lord to claim the purpose and the promise of the Joy he gives us.

Henri Nouwen wrote:

> 'We have to **CHOOSE** Joy and **KEEP** choosing it.'

June 7th

We also have to learn to 'listen with the ear of the heart' (St Benedict) if we are to be of any real utility to God.

Have words and walk past a beggar. Have words yet carry on regardless. Have words and leap in without thinking when our Saviour is being defamed.

Surely, we should be rushing to the defence of the impoverished not God, he's heard it all before.

Or in my case, have words and mutter away to myself incessantly and inadequately and keep walking.

June 8th

There has been another massive shooting in an American school. What troubled minds perpetrate such mayhem and misery? It is beyond our experience in UK for the most part, thank God. How can we keep a mentoring eye on the youngsters in our communities? How can we quietly help them to find the self-respect and self-worth needed to mature into viable, valuable citizens of the world?

Good Lord, as the tear ravaged faces of frightened students and parents fill the news I pray that good and light will somehow triumph over such wanton destruction of lives and futures. I pray that through the horror, despite the horror, young folk will find a collective honouring of goodness and respectability.   Amen.

June 9th

In continuing to pray for the friends and families of the students lost yesterday I realise again how destructive polarisation and denominational labelling is. How, whilst categorisation is seen as the rational template by which a society is sorted and sifted, many are left feeling disenfranchised and alone. How can we ever hope to reach out to these hurting people *before* they not only self-destruct but take dozens of innocents with them?

June 10th

I am writing these next few days up from notes I made whilst away visiting friends and in doing so am receiving a double helping of blessing. There was much fun and laughter, tasty food and music during our visit and now as I re-read though my hastily jotted diary I get to relive and remember the goodness all over again. I sometimes feel sad that I don't live near enough to this particular friend to be able to share a quick cup of coffee or the occasional glass of wine. How much sweeter and more special is our time together when it does happen and how lovely to be able to relax into each other's company for an unhurried reunion.

June 11th

A day catching up with my friend's children and grandchildren, precious additions who have all become as family to me. They are so generous with their open love and pleasure in being able spend time with me and, through their teasing and 'joshing' make me feel how deeply they all love me. What a privilege. Thank you for their generosity Lord help me never to take these things for granted.

June 12th

A girls' day out. First to Gloucester Cathedral to see an exhibition of illuminated manuscripts, and the treasured chance to sit in quiet prayerfulness with someone for whom I pray every day, as I know she does me. We have been praying for each other and our families since we were starting our married lives together and through many storms in tea cups and bathtubs we have had our faith to furnish and nourish each other. As yesterday's prayer, Lord help me never to take her for granted, bless, guard, guide and keep her close to you.

June 13th

Rubbish journey home, just to prove that one can't sit on a cloud of loveliness for too long in this life, that a bubble will pop, that contentment is only a veneer intact so long as everything is going well.
Grrrrrrrrrrr traffic.
Rubbish?? The only rubbish is me. I am letting this journey undo so much of God's grace and bounty that we have all received over the past few days. I am pricking my bubble, I am turning something deeply restorative into a pickable veneer.
Father forgive me. I am sorry.

June 14th

Many of my friends know that for many years I have been involved in prayer ministry, either as a participant in groups or as a practitioner trying to share and encourage others to explore, deepen and develop their prayer life. Had I had a pound for every time someone had said to me 'I don't know how to pray' I would be a major benefactor of many projects.

Jesus said, when asked by the disciples about prayer, Matthew 6:9–13, just say 'Our Father.......' and although therein lies all we actually need to say there are times and situations when we feel we would like to do more, with Lectio Divina or a picture or an icon or through the warming light of a candle flame; times when learning to sit in silence and centre to an inward, still place is transformative.

'I don't know how to pray'; don't like silence; wouldn't be able to stay focussed on a candle flame; haven't got an icon. No? so start by writing to God. It is amazing how stuff just pours out when we sit with a pen and paper. Feeling unthreatened and uncensored, in the safety of our own space, prayer will happen.

June 15th

Of course, prayer isn't all about deeply engineered times of stillness and reflection. Walking our daughter's dog across the fields in the early morning or late evening can be as meditative as any monastic cell. Singing hymns as I do the ironing can have the twofold effect, of praising my Lord whilst making a dull task almost pleasurable. I did say 'almost'. Living thankfully as the day develops is also prayer if God is acknowledged and given the glory. Our New Age brothers and sisters call it Mindfulness and now boast of it as the answer to all one's inner stresses. I rather think we people of faith have been doing it a tad longer...read the psalms. Ps 145 v2 'Every day I shall bless you and praise your name, for ever and ever'. Ps 147 'Acknowledge the Lord for all the day.' Amen.

June 16th

I had a flyer from the bank the other day promising me huge benefits if I open a new savings account. Pah! where is there one of those to be found these days?
A promise worth having I do know about though,
'For it is written, He shall give his angels charge over thee to keep thee. In their hands, they shall bear thee up lest at any time you dash your foot upon a stone'. Luke 4: 10-11
Glad I'm a fully signed up member for that.

June 17th

It's hot, hot, dry and utterly perfect – for me at any rate. I feel the cold radically.
I love the heat, I can take any amount of it. I remember being in Las Vegas some years ago and the digital thermometer on the outside of a building was reading 105 degree Fahrenheit. My husband turned to me, took my face in his hands and said, 'Please darling tell me you're warm enough?'
I was, and I have to work very hard at being patient when, in our temperate climate here in northern Europe, people start to voice their discomfort at the first of a precious few decent days. I try to smile and sympathise but it is two faced of me because inside I'm rejoicing.
Today is glorious, thank you, you great big beautiful God of sunshine.

June 18th

Still lovely weather though some rain forecast for around tea time. It's easy to use the sunshine and showers scenario as a metaphor for life, it's been done to death. The weather does influence so much of our wellbeing though and I might have seemed harsh yesterday, dismissive even of those who feel compromised by the heat, if so, I'm sorry. I do know many people who suffer from the now clinically accepted condition called SAD (Seasonally Affected Disease), those for whom the grey dark days of winter settle a blanket of general gloom over their outlook on life and make every day a slog.

I am blessed to be on the optimistic side of the outlook spectrum, my family often tease me for my 'Pollyanna' outlook on the world and so today as I revel in another glorious summer day, I pray for those whose lives are more complicated and those for whom it isn't merely a matter of weather that sets the tone of their coping.

June 19th

My bible notes have asked me an interesting question

'When have you heard God's voice from an unexpected source?'
The more I think about this, the more I need to think about it.

June 20th

Perhaps I have been too analytical, perhaps years of deciphering every nuanced phrase in student essays has left me unable to read things at page value but that question had me pondering all day.

To **'hear'** means I was complicit in the action, when did I **hear,** not just acknowledge in passing or retrospectively, **when** did I 'hear'. **When?** This assumes it was sufficiently momentous for me to register it. **'God's voice',** something clearly discernible from any other conversation or thought process. Then, from an **'unexpected source'.** Could I claim the beauty of the morning dew in a spider's web or should I try to be more literal and answer the question more philosophically. Or am I being too pedantic and yes God's voice can be through an image. Clearly, I'm not going to have the full oral delivery straight from inside a cloud.

However, I am being asked a direct question about a direct experience, not something open to semantics. An 'unexpected source' throws a definite caveat into the question. I can hear the voice of God daily as I speak and pray with my Christian friends and colleagues.... but......?

I am now trying to actively connect and be more thoughtfully aware, although, if I look for and identify the source it won't then be unexpected, will it?

June 21st

Of course, there is the story of the drowned man who when he got to the pearly gates berated God for not hearing his cries for help.

'What do you mean?' replied God

'I sent a guy with a life belt, you sent him away. I sent the life boat, you sent it away. I sent a rescue helicopter, you sent it away.'

I hope the dead guy was suitably shame faced, as I need to be for all the times I miss hearing God's voice in the unexpected, unrecognised and ordinary times and places.

June 22nd

It's still lovely weather, not as hot as it has been but more comfortable and 'English'. I was talking with a neighbour who has very sore bones, but her arthritis is eased when she can sit in the sunshine.

> Sore bones, bent and twisted into knotted puzzles
> across many painful winters, wake in the sun's warmth,
> fingers and toes, hips and knees feel the breath
> of solar life start to soften thickened, toughened joints.
> The choreography of unaffected movement can never be revisited
> but small dextrous freedoms are celebrated and a heartfelt
> 'Thank you, Sunshine,' offered.
> Medicine comes in many forms.

June 23rd

I've been making vast quantities of tomato soup for the freezer from the huge crop we've had and I know, when we tuck into it in the autumn, we will really feel the goodness of summer filling us with liquid sunshine.
Thank you for the plants Lord. Thank you for the time to make the soup Lord. Thank you for a freezer to enable us to enjoy this later.

June 24th

Cardinal Newman wrote a prayer called 'God' and it makes a wonderful week's readings.

Verse 1

'God has created me to do Him some definite service. He has committed some work to me which He has not committed to another. I have my mission -I many never know it in this life, but I shall be told it in the next.'

I think that I must strive always to do and say only what is pleasing to the Lord irrespective of audience, time or place...quite a challenge.

June 25th

Verse 2

'I am a link in a chain, a bond of connection between persons. He has not created me for naught. I shall do good, I shall do his work.'

I think I am being told that it's OK to ask for help, I don't need to do everything on my own to prove what a good and capable person I am, which in any case I'm not. Involving others is good for me, from them and the strength of the whole.

June 26th

Verse 3

'I shall be an angel of peace, a preacher of truth in my own place whilst not intending it, if I do but keep His commandments.'

I think the 'whilst not intending it' must mean that if I am doing the Lords will and living the Gospel message daily that peace and truth will become an intrinsic part of who I am. Lord there's a long way to go but change and mould me please.

June 27th

Verse 4
'Therefore I will trust Him. Whatever and wherever I am. I can never be thrown away. If I am in sickness, my sickness may serve Him; if I'm in sorrow, my sorrow can serve Him. He does nothing in vain, He knows what he is about. He may take away my friends, thrown me among strangers, He may make me feel desolate, make my spirits sink, hide my future from me, still He knows what He is about.'
What HUGE promise and comfort these words hold on days when I feel things are dragging me down.

June 28th

These past four days have brought me right back to the essence of what it means to call myself a Christian. Fundamental, unadorned truths about my responsibilities and God's promises. No denominational dressing, no socio-political or politically correct interpretation, just me before the throne of God, before the mercy seat.
What a journey:
'The person who is put right with God through faith shall live.'   Romans 1: 17

June 29th

I am not doing anything today. I have a whole empty day in my calendar. I've had a slow start with breakfast in my pj's and the paper, followed by a bath rather than a hasty, barely damp shower. Now I'm sitting at my computer with a cup of coffee and feeling guilty that I have no specifically assigned tasks or deadline to meet. I ought to be doing extra bible study, I ought be having an extra-long time of prayer, I ought not to waste a moment.
I think I'm suffering from '*clogged up **oughteries***'.
Father whatever I end up doing I know you walk beside me.

June 30th

Why, after all these years am I surprised? Call it serendipity, call it fate or, recognise the grace of God acting through a friend not seen for a while who rings up and suggests the pictures. A new film that I wanted to see but knew Peter wouldn't want to.
Film followed by supper.
God bless my friend and help me to be a good friend too.

July 1st

I don't talk much about our caravan. Yes, they are a real pain on the lanes if you get behind one. We love ours though.

Many people know that my dear younger sister Brenda, her husband and two little boys died in a caravan accident when they suffocated from carbon monoxide poisoning during a winter skiing holiday. Yes, it was a black, bleak time and for many years I was not inclined to even step inside one let alone consider owning one again.

Time heals as they say and after a twenty-year gap, the expansion of our family and the arrival of our grandchildren we began to remember the wonderful family holidays we had enjoyed with our brood and we decided to put a toe back in water, on the understanding if I really couldn't cope we'd sell up again. Suffice to say that was six years ago and we haven't looked back. In prayerful trust, we initially embarked on short trips to fairly local sites and eventually moved on to a nine-week tour of Europe to celebrate our retirement. Children and families have borrowed the van and we are now getting ready to take our youngest grandson away for the first time.

He hasn't been away on his own before but he does know and love the caravan so we are all excited and looking forward to a blessed, happy time. In trust, we know we'll be fine but I am going to enlist some support from my amazingly faithful prayer partners.

July 2nd

How special are some people? A girl friend, when I asked for some prayer cover for our holiday, offered to come over and actually sit and pray with me in the caravan, she also reminded me of the promise in Ps 139:2-3 'You have searched me out and know my sitting down and my standing up, you discern my fears from afar. You mark out my journeys and my resting place and are acquainted with all my ways.' I am so often knocked out by the love of my friends and surprised by the joy and grace with which they do things. I am truly blessed.

July 3rd

Does the fact that I never expect generosity from friends and colleagues mean that somehow, I don't really value them in my life? It's a harsh thought and one I instinctively fight against, and what's more I don't feel I can identify with, but does 'familiarity breeds contempt' have any resonance? Perish the thought but I believe that this is another flash input from the Lord to just put me on my metal and make sure that I try to treat everyone, always with the mind of Jesus.

July 4th

I read on through Ps 139 and found the line:
 'If I take the wings of the morning'
and thought what a lovely waking up mantra that would be, before my head is even off the pillow.
Lord I take the wings of this morning, the promise of this day and fly out into the world knowing that I am clothed in your renewing Holy Spirit, that my brokenness is made whole through you, High King of Heaven. Amen.

July 5th

I started to look for things to put into a charity collection bag which came through the letter box a few days ago. I missed the last date because I kept putting off what I knew would be a big task and so I am determined not to be such a procrastinator this time. Oh but what a shameful amount of stuff I have. I'm not apologising for things I wear and enjoy wearing but there's a lot of items that haven't seen the light for a few seasons. Come on Irena, wear it or share it!

Hey, I like that tag line, perhaps I should laminate it and stick it inside my wardrobe.

July 6th

Jesus fed the five thousand. Whether through encouraging people to share or a hugely divine miracle over the loaves and fishes, whatever, an enormous number of people were fed and with food left over. I'm not being disrespectful but I make an analogy with my sorting out yesterday, the extra bags I needed to use and the fact that I am still not in danger of having to go out half dressed. I am really embarrassed at how many T shirts there were, and pairs of jeans, and shirts from a now redundant working wardrobe of clothes, and jackets, oh and socks! when did I buy so many pairs of socks? many unworn.

I think this kind of exercise is supposed to be cathartic but I'm just rather ashamed at my profligacy. I've promised myself I will be more thoughtful before I buy something new another time.........

but will I?

July 7th

The Lord doesn't want my second-hand anything! He demands the best.
'All things come from God and of his own do we give Him' - we say this every time we celebrate the Eucharist. God is only ever capable of giving the best to us but 'of His own do we give Him', really?
Do I give Him back in anything like the measure He gives to me?
Sadly, pathetically, wilfully, thoughtlessly, stubbornly, deliberately, no, nowhere near.

July 8th

I can *rejoice* though and I can sit at my piano and play through Mission Praise and my mother's old copy of the Methodist hymn book. I can play and sing to my heart content, not sure about my poor husband's hearing and patience but a few hymns do my soul no end of good.
I guess that's why after all these years 'Songs of Praise', every Sunday evening on the BBC, hasn't been axed. I'm sure the men in suits at the Beeb have tried but I imagine the outpouring of very strong, passionate viewer opinion is what has kept the programme running since October 1961. That would be impressive for any broadcast but for a religious one it is spectacular.

July 9th

I was singing at a wedding service today, just a voice co-opted to swell our church choir on special occasions and I was aware of two things, firstly the togetherness of singing and the uplifting feel-good factor of singing with others, also the immense privilege of helping to make a wedding day special for the couple and congregation.

Today's couple were from Christian families for whom the sacramental part of the service was very important and for whom the vows and hand of God on their union was fundamental to the whole celebration. The readings were chosen with theological emphasis as were the hymns and it was a truly joyous occasion full of meaning and symbolism.

Everyone's wedding day ought to be unique and exceptional but having been singing at weddings now for a year I can tell, blindfold, which are the nuptials where there is a live faith and which are the formalities for a 'white wedding'.

July 10th

Does what we wear to church matter? Some of the brides this summer have been quite 'forthcoming' in their choice of wedding dress and we have seen many very low-cut bodices and uncovered arms. I'm not passing an opinion, merely asking if perhaps there is an expected appropriacy when in church. Gone are the suits and ties of my childhood, sweaters and jeans are very normal at the all age family services where informality is the preferred way but does this relaxed attitude enable people to reach God more easily and in fact *should* that be the fostered attitude?

Does this dress-down dress code make the angry God of the Old Testament a softer option? Does it show less respect than if we were all still putting on the 'Sunday Best' week by week?

Of course, it is what's in our hearts that the good Lord sees and responds to, but just as I try to make an effort for lunch with friends or family, just as I make an effort when I'm at the hospital on my chaplaincy day, just as I would get togged up to visit the Queen, so I feel it incumbent upon me to make an effort for my King of Kings?

I know this makes sound like a dinosaur.

July 11th

More asylum seekers drowned.

OUTRAGE

Outrage at people dying at sea but
how dare the media bring their misery to me
in the comfort of my own home?
How dare the media broadcast the images
of pathetic, frightened people, hungry and cold
young and old seeking freedom
when I'm eating my supper?
How dare they look so determined and brave
in the face of abject abuse and desperation
when I can take for granted my comfort and lack of
anything too much to stress about?
Apart that is from worrying about the endless tide
of humanity being unceremoniously
washed up on the beach, out of reach of
their oppressors, for now, until like reject fish
they are tossed back to take their chance
and wait for the next tide.

July 12th

This problem is bigger than me or any one person. We can pray, we do pray, most earnestly, as if an earnest prayer is more acceptable to God than any other heartfelt intercession. We can petition governments and ruling bodies, NGOs and charities but where will the solution come from in the end? I know the adage that for evil to succeed good men need only do nothing but what can be done? The perpetrators of injustices on a humanitarian scale like never before, need to be brought down but then, like apple-bobbing another even worse one seems to come to the surface to claim the crown of evil, megalomaniac, despot.

Father God, my guilt at my plenty isn't going to help anyone unless there is something I can do to translate guilt into action. If there is something that I'm not already committed to please show me.

July 13th

Another friend of ours is terminally ill just now and we feel impotent to be of any practical use. The family is closed in around their pain and they are savouring every day of their loved one's time with them but the guilt thing is there again. This time because we are both in good health. Is guilt a useless emotion really, does it just lead to a form of inverse self-pity?

It is obviously inappropriate to bound around like 'Tigger' celebrating one's good fortune, health and happiness; it seems disingenuous to walk about clothed in righteous solemnity and sepulchral respect. What is the right thing to do? Yes, just be 'normal'. Outwardly that's fine but it doesn't stop the inner turmoil.

CS Lewis wrote: 'Experience: that most brutal of teachers. But you learn, my God do you learn.'

Help me to learn Father God.

July 14th

Just finished reading 'The Little Coffee Shop of Kabul' by Deborah Rodriguez, a real little gem.

What an amazing insight into life in one of the most troubled places on earth, yet, troubles apart, a demonstration of the triumph of women's human spirit. When have I ever had to really fight for anything?

Burqa clad, anonymous, faceless, their bodies shuffle across the newsreels and no gender awareness or characterisation is accredited to them but after reading this book I will think more about the fighting, beating hearts of mothers and sisters and grandmothers, all wanting the best for their families just like I do except, for them, in the most extenuating circumstances.

July 15th

So, with all my good intentions of yesterday, trusting and being less judgmental etc etc. I found myself surveying with suspicion a rucksack left on its own in the cathedral and seeing a group of Asians assumed it was theirs, which of course it wasn't. I kept my fleeting thoughts to myself, realised to whom it belonged and asked her to please keep it with her, even as she knelt in prayer.

All I can think is 'Thank you Lord for putting the brakes on any ignorant, impetuous action I might have taken.'

I am ashamed.

July 16th

Mary said:
'My heart praises the Lord; my soul is glad because of God my saviour,
For he has remembered me, his lowly servant;
from now on all people will call me blessed because of the great things the
Lord has done for me.'   Luke 1: 48

It wasn't pride when Mary said that all people would call her blessed, it
wasn't a 'God chose me over you', reaction. Quite the reverse, she was
recognising and accepting the gift from God without demur or false
modesty.
Pride would be in turning down a gift as though it wasn't good enough
whilst knowing the opposite. That is just bad grace and makes the giver of a
gift or compliment feel very uncomfortable but why it is hard to just accept
something given in love with no hidden agenda, a gift or compliment?

July 17th

Phew, Scorchio, glorious day, but a bit grumpy because I must be indoors.
Double grumpy because it's my own fault that have to be indoors, helping
to sort out some overstuffed and junk filled rooms in the old scout shed.
My fault because I thought I would be missing something if I didn't get
involved with the other 'girls'. Even more grumpy that I never seem to
learn my lesson. Ah well, here goes.

July 18th

After a very busy but hugely productive morning yesterday, with rooms cleared and a stack of bin bags of rubbish and other bags for the tip or the charity shop, someone suggested a bar snack.

We had a couple of hours of fun and fellowship whilst being regaled by one of the group who was for many years a guide leader. The various trysts and assignations she had discovered in those corners and cubby holes would make an interesting read, material not just from the youngsters either! Certainly, there were several empty bottles hidden deep under piles of 'stuff' and a couple of half packets of contraband cigarettes.

Grump to gratitude; might I have learned a lesson?

July 19th

'Ignorance Divides' A headline I saw on a (supposedly) Christian publication. I didn't buy it so I didn't read the article but it left me pondering for a long time.

Yes, ignorance does or at least can divide. A stance taken in an uninformed situation is clearly going to be ignorance in action.

I think it's the interpretation of the word 'ignorance' which is my problem. When it is being used pejoratively, insinuating that one opinion is of less worth than another, then isn't that in itself ignorant?

We live in politically turbulent times and it is surely more important than ever that we opine from positions of knowledge and insight, not just emotion and self-importance.

True knowledge doesn't necessarily close the gap on opposing ideologies therefore there will always be a schism even when either side is in full possession of all the relevant information, ergo no longer in 'ignorance' but perhaps a more sure foundation for the discussion can be acknowledged.

July 20th

I was still picking way at yesterday's thoughts and praying for clarity this morning then, whilst I was having my breakfast, absentmindedly listening to the radio, I heard about a new multi-faith initiative in Manchester. The place name interested me immediately since we have family and emotional ties to the city but it struck me that here was an explanation to my 'Ignorance Divides' conundrum.

I have studied comparative religion and so know a little of Hinduism, Islam, Bahia and Zoroastrianism.

I am not 'ignorant' about them but I am divided from them by choice not to partake.

So perhaps it was still a harsh headline for a Christian publication in my opinion, suggesting that once well informed on a subject we would all be on the same side of whatever debate.

Where is this Utopia? Not this side of heaven.

July 21st

After a couple of days skimming the pond of philosophical examination I am thankful that days of extended academic discourse and debate are no longer the centre of my universe. So, I am going for a picnic.

I have phoned a few local friends I haven't seen for a while, suggested we meet with our lunch at the country park and I am looking forward to it.

Father God thank you for this day, thank you for my friends and their obvious joy at my suggestion, thank you for the country park and, well, just a great big THANK YOU.

July 22nd

Thank you again Lord for yesterday. For the blessing of friends and shared love and commitment to one another, help me never to take them for granted.

As we ate one of the group looked at her bread roll and said, 'The Bread of the Presence'. I thought she was reminding us that at our picnic, there with us, was the Lord and indeed she was. I asked though about her use of words and she referred me to 1 Samuel 21:6 where I later learned that once a week, on the Sabbath, a priest entered the Holy Place in the tabernacle and placed 12 freshly baked loaves of bread on a small table. This bread was called the 'Bread of the Presence' and symbolised God's presence among his people and his commitment to them and their physical needs as well as in that place.

There are many symbols of faith around our home but I really love the thought of a roll or piece of bread put out fresh every day as my personal proclamation, prayer and acknowledgment of 'The Presence', His Presence, God's Presence.

July 23rd

The day-old bread, yes I did it yesterday, I put a slice of bread, (I didn't have any fresh baked rolls) on a plate on the counter top in the kitchen. It was a very comforting gesture and strangely more meaningful than some of the more precious keepsakes and mementoes in my study. Perhaps I have become complacent about the lovely icon, perhaps I no longer really see the olive wood cross from Jerusalem, maybe I no longer notice the prayer picture apart from when it accompanies me on retreat. However, that slice of bread was like a hug every time I went into the kitchen, it was very special and this morning I fed it to the birds so it was still used to the glory of God.

I don't think I'm going to do it every day because I don't want it to lose its impact but I will certainly share it amongst my friends in faith.

July 24th

Almost without fail, when I have had a taste of true peace in meditation, or a time of precious loveliness with others, within no time at all someone or something comes along with a big pin to burst the bubble.

Times without number this happens. Is it fate? Is it a manifestation of a malign presence hating the joy my faith brings to me? I could dwell on it but I won't because I shrug it off as 'life'. The plain truth is that this side of Glory I must share my time and space with seven billion people on this earth, all with their own agendas, agonies, lives, loves, hatreds, hungers and prayers, to my God, their God, deities and idols.

Why then should I expect my state of peace to remain untouched?

Am I really so shallow or am I just human?

That's life.

July 25th

Father God
Plant in me a thought, a prayer,
a word, some silence, I don't care
what form your presence takes, just
so long as it makes me know you.
Plant then nurture your chosen
mode of knowing until I recognise
your hand in its fruitfulness and
submit to your season.
Temper my inclination to
impetuous rushing, outgrowing
my capabilities before your
time and until then hold me in
gentle, measured wholeness.
Plant in my identity a
strong familial likeness, traits of
genus Christian that make me know
you claim me and others to recognise
my creator.

July 26th

We are going off in the caravan for a few days, off up to Northumberland to be with the family and as always, I'm full of anticipation as we start to load up.

We sleep incredibly well although everything is in miniature and on the face of it should be claustrophobic and, because space is at a premium we seem to achieve a level of tidiness that would be enviable at home.

Bring on the evening glass of wine and then bacon sandwiches for breakfast, oh and a new book I've been longing to read.

July 27th

I confess to three days missed in my journal. A six-year-old grandson to be entertained doesn't leave much time for self during the day and because we have a shocking habit of flouting family/house rules in the caravan, bed time wasn't far from our own.

We did make a wonderful 'Rubbishbot' over the three days. Two cardboard boxes, a cheap beach ball and rubbish gathered throughout the day resulted in a very fine creation with kitchen roll tube arms, one old rubber glove hand and the other a picnic plate satellite receiver. Egg box battery packs all down his back and sundry finds decorating the front, miles of duct tape and a can of bright blue car spray all meant that a very fine 'project' was taken home.

Happy exhaustion…all of us.

July 28th

There was a lovely river running though the camp site and Peter spent a fair bit of time with Charlie building dams, were ever two lads happier?

He also taught Charlie how to skim, firstly how to select the perfect stone and then how to hold it correctly to be able to flick the spin as it is let fly. Rather a lot for little six-year-old hands to manage but he tried and tried and tried some more and was beyond thrilled when the first double then triple bounce occurred. The disappointment when it didn't work was abject but often as much because he hadn't taken the time to select the right stone and just lobbed any old lump into the water.

Thank God that He doesn't look for the most perfect specimens on which to lavish his love and attention.

Thank God, we can all fit into his hands whatever size or shape and above all, thank God that we will never be spun off with a flick of the divine wrist.

July 29th

Summerful England,
what lovelier, totally
wholesomely lovely place is
there to remember a
totally, wholesomely
lovely world.
To recognise, to appreciate,
to celebrate,
to be content with
what we have,
not what we want,
where we are
not where we'd prefer to be.
To stand, eyes closed
on the pavement or
the grass, face turned up to
feel the sun.
Summerful England
part of this amazing
beautiful, sad,
spinning ball of rock,
Thank you.

July 30th

On a church notice board in Northumberland we read (names changed)
Vicar James Broad
Lay reader Ann West
Ministers All of us.
All of us. ALL OF US. ALL OF US. **ALL OF US.**

July 31st

Perhaps it is worth remembering a quotation from the great polymath and philosopher Frederick Nietzsche
'Christians will have to LOOK redeemed if I am to believe in a redeemer'.

Ministers, '**All of Us**' even just by the faces we present to the world.

August 1st

Just how can I do that all the time? I can manage on the days when I feel sunny but what about the days when for no explicable reason, I waken up out of sorts, grumpy, less than positive. Maybe for no good reason, maybe because some item on the breakfast news has rattled me. Irritation too when something seems too simplistic or trite in my bible notes and so with which I disagree mightily.

Perhaps I am becoming an old curmudgeon. Ah some might say knowingly 'becoming?'

I don't think I am naturally irascible, I know I'm not.

So, what face do I present to the world on a day to day basis? How do I look 'redeemed'?

Not by smiling inanely as I walk to get the paper and milk but certainly by smiling openly and saying hello or good morning when I meet people. By taking the extra nanosecond to ask after someone or comment on their dog and yes this might develop into rather more of an exchange than I had wanted but if in that time, the person of Jesus can be manifest somehow through this 'old boot' that's a result. That's the face of redemption.

Further to living an active faith without words, it's there in Matthew 25:37:

'Lord when did we see you hungry and feed you, or thirsty and give you something to drink? When did we see you a stranger and invite you in or need clothes and clothe you? When did we see you sick or in prison and visit you? And the Lord replied: "I tell you the truth, whatever you did for the least of one of these brothers of mine you did for me".'

Do I do it often enough? Do I do it unbidden? Could I do it better?

August 2nd

Well who knew it? I've got telomeres and, what's more, I can influence them and their effect on me.

I thought that a salad, plenty of fruit and loads of vitamin D through this glorious sunshine was enough but Oh no!

Here's the science; chromosomes carry genetic information, I knew that much, but at their tips are strands of DNA called telomeres, a bit like the plastic ends on shoe laces to stop them fraying.

Theses telomeres are there to protect my genetic data from deteriorating, which happens when the said telomeres shorten and fray also, lifestyle and mental health state can accelerate the process.

Cholesterol, blood pressure, BMR, resting heart rate, now telomeres! I could increase my stress levels just trying to balance, evaluate and maintain the status quo I have now and that's before the day has really got going.

Father God my trust is in you.

August 3rd

Clearly my reading and research from yesterday's discovery took the best part of the day and I have been persuaded that, without being complacent, I'm doing most of the right things. Even the red wine is okay.

Could I however, try to restore any damage to my telomeres was my main concern and yes apparently, I can. It is within my power to slow the cellular rate at which I'm aging. I feel a trumpet voluntary coming on.

Clearly, I need to stop my DNA ends from unravelling by having strong telomeres and the longer the better. If they shorten too far they will eventually die and then my DNA will just unravel away taking me with it until everything is broken and I die.

Keeping a sense of perspective though I am happy to know that I can influence things, it isn't too late to forestall the elements that might have a quantifiable effect.

Being aware of the areas that cause stress and how one deals with them is a huge influence also a positive rather than a negative outlook, generally speaking, I'm an optimistic person. Also, a fair to middling self-image seems to be important, be kind to yourself I read, and be open rather than suspicious to others because meeting a conversation with one's guard up does something to one's cortisol levels which is detrimental. Cortisol, what's cortisol?..............................I'm going in the garden.

August 4th

I distanced myself from self-destructive, stress inducing, telomere shortening thoughts and decided to visit a wonderful, very old, very infirm Christian lady whom I have been privileged to get to know.

She is well read and very well informed on current affairs, up to date on what's happening in the various TV thrillers and serials, knows her bible, chapter and verse, literally, and radiates the love of Christ, I want to hug her. All this from her bed and chair clutching her beloved iPad, she is a wiz with it. Her granddaughter got her up and running and if ever there was something to celebrate in the advances of the internet and WWW she is it. I bet her telomeres are the longest and strongest ever.

'Darling, how wonderful to see you' she greets me, and I suspect everyone, with her arms out-stretched for an embrace, though she is so frail to apply any pressure would cause her pain. 'Come and tell me everything you've been doing' she then encourages, never ever mentioning her ongoing discomforts, physical treatments or mentally exhausting fights with social services.

I love her, we all do. When she prays, which she does regularly throughout the visit, unbidden and out of the blue, it is always so eloquent, sincere and simple that it takes one straight through the front door of heaven.

She doesn't need my prayers, the good Lord has her wrapped in a huge duvet of his presence.

August 5th

Watching the children playing yesterday afternoon I was transported to my own tent making days. The clothes horse, we called it a 'maiden' don't know why, was erected on its side and an old blanket thrown over and adventures were had hour after hour.

Now they have a real tent which just shakes out and self erects into a big dome but the fun they were having was every bit as wonderful and ended in a free for all as they tried to get as many as they could in there.

I know I take it out of context but I remembered the verse from Isaiah 54:2:

'Enlarge the place of your tent, stretch your tent curtain wide, do not hold back, lengthen your cords and strengthen your stakes.'

A semblance of peace was restored when biscuits and juice arrived and somehow all the little people fitted in, sitting down, for their picnic.

We used to have jam and bread.

August 6th

There is so much turbulence in the world that I feel my musings probably seem shallow and inconsequential. I know though, from my Coffee Pot Journal, that although ordinary and uncomplicated many, many people have told me how on a particular day something spoke directly to them.

When I sit to write I ask that the Lord be my guide and inspiration as I share the events of my days.

I have written political letters and pieces to the papers and government bodies across the years and continue to do so but I don't feel this is the place for ideological tub-thumping. I guess I am trying to make my own, albeit overtly Christian, safe space to knock a few thoughts and ideas around, to share some precious moments, to gently raise a few issues, without being unnecessarily shrill or forceful or 'In yer face' as they say.

Sure, the world is in ferment, it always was but we must have faith that God is in charge and just because *we* can't see a solution or make everything better immediately doesn't mean that we should lose hope and stop trying.

August 7th

Luke 6:34-39 lays the rule bare I think:
'Do not judge and you won't be judged.
Do not condemn and you won't be condemned.
Forgive and you will be forgiven.
Give and it will be given to you.
A good measure pressed down, shaken together and running over
will be poured into your lap, for with the measure
you use it will be measured to you.'

Memo to self: Two ears, one mouth and I need to apologise to someone before today is over.

August 8th

When someone is gracious and kind, generous and forgiving towards one, ie me, whose impulsiveness caused discomfort and embarrassment, it makes one, ie me, feel even more ashamed and relieved that my apology has been accepted.

August 9th

When I ask for forgiveness in my prayers and truly repent and sincerely mean what I say, why does the knowledge of the Lord's total loving absolution not feel as powerful as when another human being bestows it?
Yet I know it is without agenda, without strings, just a complete washing away of my sin leaving me as good as new in His eyes.
Seventy times seven, that's an incomprehensible amount of forgiving.

August 10th

Summer rain, glorious rain, thank God rain.
But the media is moaning.
'It won't do any good,' 'The ground is too hard,' 'Still a need to water,'
I KNOW, I KNOW! it's been very dry. I KNOW there are huge problems
because of the drought.
I also know that some folks live like this for years not a few weeks.
Can I please, for now, in my own little bubble, be happy for this lovely rain?

August 11th

I'm still sad and embarrassed at my thoughtfulness of a few days ago, why
don't I feel more forgiven? Then, last night I read:
    'There is vanity in excess penance.'
An observation on the extreme lives of Fathers, Martyrs and Saints by an
unnamed recusant.
Point being, time I got over it and moved on.

August 12th

A plastic sheet and a hose pipe equals hours of endless fun and the shrieks
and whoops of happiness banish every negative thought about economics,
politics, councils and corporations.
Children's ability to centre and restore one is remarkable and yes, all the
worrisome, grown up stuff is there, it hasn't gone away but the brief respite
from having to be constantly bombarded by the awfulness of the world at
large has helped me to see goodness, to hear kindness, to know the beauty
of the moment. To take and treasure that beauty. To let that moment be
oil on the troubled waters of my mind.

August 13th

I wish we knew more about Jesus as a child. Watching the children yesterday larking about and laughing till they were helpless I feel sure that he too would have played, but then when I think that at the age of 12 he sat with the teachers and scholars in the temple in Jerusalem, I can't see it.

He was already, by that age, aware of the issues and philosophies of contemporary thought sufficient to sit amongst the teachers, asking questions and amazing them with his intelligence. The reply to his distraught parents when they found him comes over as rather obnoxious, yet totally accepting, even then, of the life mapped out for him. See Luke 2: 41-50

He must have played, surely?

August 14th

Play is still uppermost in my mind.

I watched grown-ups playing tennis yesterday evening and shared the triumphs and disasters of aces and nets, of deuces and tie breaks. It was a thoroughly good natured local match with another club and although at times the banter seemed harsh; it was, in the truest sense, a time of community spirit. Perhaps we adults should 'play out' together more often, there would be squabbles – bad line calls maybe – but a few hours of physical recreation and we all went home feeling better for it. We can't all go to Wimbledon or Twickenham, Wembley or Lords but there is joy to be found at very local levels and at a fraction of the price.

August 15th

'A wicked man is trapped by his own words but an honest man gets himself out of trouble.' Prov.12:13

'No matter how much a lazy person may want something, he will never get it. A hard worker will get everything he wants.' Prov. 13:4

And sometimes the wisdom of the Book of Proverbs seems counterintuitive or even downright wrong when I read in the press about how bad people seem to go from strength to strength and the underdogs become even more downtrodden.

I have to believe that God *will* have the final say and justice prevail but I wish I could be around to see some of the 'evil-doers' get their comeuppance.

August 16th

'Trouble follows sinners everywhere but righteous people will be rewarded with good things.' Prov. 13:21

For all the truly lovely, kind, faithful people who seem to get bad luck and upset at every turn, whose families are a constant source of fighting, whose health issues are immense, whose financial situation goes from worrying to parlous; how can they not laugh in the face of this verse?

They wouldn't be human if they didn't question the truth of these words as they struggle on and watch the real sinners go from success to success, the unpleasant characters with no moral compass seemingly surging ahead.

But then, the truly lovely, kind, faithful people are just that, and show me how carrying on in faith is a far greater testament to the love of God than writing about odious comparisons.

August 17th

'Though He slay me, yet will I trust Him.'   Job 13: 15
How often does it happen? Confirmation of a greater head, heart and hand than mine at work.
That was this morning's text from my on-line thought for the day and it brings me back to **TRUST**.
Trust and Obey.
Will I ever learn?

August 18th

It's hot, it's mid-week and I'm retired so I am going to sit in the shade and read.
Nothing erudite, nothing scriptural or spiritual but what I hope will be a thumping good murder mystery with plenty of forensic science detail.
Thank you for this day and the opportunity to use it just for me.

August 19th

I shouldn't write my daily log in the morning.
You know what they say about how to make God laugh, tell him your plans.
So, yesterday, mug of coffee and book at the ready I answered the phone on my way to my promised day of self-indulgence. Ggrrrrrrrrr. Short-handed at the community coffee shop, was there any chance.........
Of course, I went and was there nearly all day.
I'm not going to set down what I'm planning for today.
9pm   Well I didn't, but I've had a lovely day and the book's a cracker.

August 20th

Show me your way Lord, not mine,
though I know that to follow your way
I won't always see where I'm going.
Show me your way Lord, but hold tight
to my hand not to save me from falling but
of wandering away from your plan.
Show me your way Lord, I don't see in the dark
all the pitfalls and traps though I think
I know the path well.
Show me in the light and the night, at rest
and at risk, in the busy and stillness,
alone or together with others,
Show me your way Lord.
                              Amen

August 21st

It isn't always easy to sit quietly in prayerful expectancy.
Sometimes a special stillness is just there and one can rest into it, lovingly, being with the Lord. At other times though, the goings-on of life make it impossible to 'centre' on Jesus.
That's when the use of a prayer aid is helpful, a candle flame or a picture on which to focus. Obviously, it isn't completely failsafe and the issues of the day will always try to overtake the space but anything which can help to draw the mind back into prayer is valuable and, with practice, may become less necessary.
Reciting a prayerful few words ie 'Show me your way Lord' repetitively, thoughtfully, slowly, until a rhythmic, abandoning of self is achieved is a way into a place of prayer and where the active involvement means there is less room for other distracting intrusions.
Show me your way Lord.

August 22nd

Another way of praying that I have just been asked about and of which I am an advocate, is using The Examen.
The Examen is a method of reviewing your day in the presence of God.
It is a time set aside for thankful reflection on where God is in your everyday life.
It has five steps.

1 Ask God for Light
    a. I want to look at my day through God's eyes not my own.
    b. Pray for the grace to understand how God is acting in your life.

2 Give Thanks
    a. The day I have just lived has been a gift from God, I'm grateful for it.
    b. Place yourself in God's presence, be aware and thankful for his great love for you.

3 Review the Day
    a. I analytically look back over the day, guided by the Holy Spirit.
    b. Recall specific instances, conversations and your feelings at the time.

4 Face up to my shortcomings
    a. Out of the above examination, to what's wrong in my life and me.
    b. Reflect on what you said, did or thought in those instances. Were you drawing closer to God or moving away?

5 Look forward to Tomorrow
    a. Ask God where I might need him more.
    b. How might you collaborate more effectively in faith, thinking of specific situations and conversations that might arise.

Close with The Lord's Prayer.

August 23rd

One thing I know and do believe, is that if we come prayerfully to God through the grace of Christ, on our knees in the garden, by the bed, in a church pew, standing waiting at the bus stop or in the supermarket queue, angry behind the wheel or peacefully on the shore of an idyllic lakeside, He is there, He is listening and He loves us for being with Him and allowing Him to be with us.

August 24th

The frustration of being a teenager isn't something we can pretend not to know about. No one alive can really say their teenage years are just a blur, that they can't remember trying to argue for more pocket money, to stay out a bit later, to go to a party – '*All* my friends are going!' and the eternal 'Aw it's not fair' cry as the stairs were banged up two at a time.
Even the most amenable must surely have had a few altercations of angst.
Then I had my own children and was reminded again of those awful years though of course it was pointed out to me often that I just didn't understand, that it was different in my day.
We got through it.
Now I am on the side-lines as my grandchildren push on those same boundaries, argue those same cases and still fling off upstairs as the finale to a lost session of verbal sparring.
Is it unfair of me to have a wry smile as I put the kettle on?

August 25th

Oh, I know Lord you must smile that wry smile at us simple mortals as we tread the same paths, make the same mistakes, push the same boundaries as others across the millennia have done.

Some of the issues are without too many consequences but others must make you cry out in anguish where we haven't learned about inequality, fairness, conciliation, respect for each other and this beautiful world.

Growing-up isn't just about calendar years.

August 26th

Growing up or growing into. Everywhere is busy with back-to-school preparations and yesterday I watched a very weary mum trying to coax a very irritable child into a school uniform jumper. The issue was the size and yes it did look several ages too big but mum was trying to turn the sleeves up, child was trying to pull them right down, thereby illustrating the discrepancy between actual size and projected growing. We have all been there and I felt for her, I felt for them both, I wanted to scoop them, up and take them for tea and cake.

Instead I wrinkled my nose at the child in sympathy and smiled kindly at the mum and felt so grateful that it wasn't me. The shoe department was the same but this time it was about style and function, school rules and peer group pressure, lots of tears and sulking going on.

What silly woman goes shopping on the last few days before the start of term anyway?

August 27th

Confession time. I realised, when I got home yesterday from my abortive shopping trip, that I didn't need what I'd gone for. I already have a black long sleeved T-shirt which I bought last autumn and had never worn, hence it was not immediately evident among the more favourite ones in the drawer.

I have more than enough of everything and when I look through my wardrobe there are things in there that I haven't worn for ages but love and things that I haven't worn for ages and never will again.

I need to get radical. So, before I stow away my summer clothes and bring out my winter togs I am going to be very analytical, strong, brave and sensible, I mean it, I did it earlier in the year and I can do it again.

August 28th

I made a start and there were some quite emotional decisions about this top or those jeans, this summer sweatshirt or those chinos.

It all became a metaphor for other areas of my life as I talked through what I was doing with myself, yes, I talk to myself all the time and no I don't think it odd.

What else do I need to get rid of, what else am I hanging onto because I haven't the heart to see it needs to be challenged, even though I know it does?

Where have I made excuses, and given inaccurate reasons for not getting involved, not necessarily in major situations but ones where I could be effective, bring something helpful or needed?

Lord, for my wastefulness with all you give to me, I am sorry.

August 29th

'How sweet are Your words to my taste, sweeter than honey in my mouth.'
Ps.119:103

As autumn approaches I look forward to porridge again for breakfast and on mine I always have a spoonful of honey. The last few winters I have spent rather a lot on Manuka honey having believed all the hype about the incredibly healthy properties it contains. Now as hot breakfast time comes around again I am beginning to read that all is not well in Honey Land, that I may have been being duped into buying an inferior amalgamation containing a very small amount of the real McCoy buffered with other cheaper variants.

What shall I do?

Yes Lord, there is truth and wholesome food in your words but what shall I put on my porridge?

August 30th

The theological elite will no doubt be appalled that I wrote that last sentence yesterday. I should perhaps have been more reverent in addressing the Lord, I should maybe more aware of my very humble status and not even dream to engage in a discussion about my quotidian dietary needs with Him. For those offended by my familiarity perhaps I should say that the reverential awe with which I contemplate the divine is tempered only by my own human interpretation and understanding of the Grace which has been bestowed upon me.

Rudolph Otto coined the word 'numinous' for the unspeakable, inexplicable holiness of Christ and I am grateful for it but I also know that Jesus, in His very humanity is the unseen guest at every meal and the friend with whom I share everything.

August 31st

Talking of food I was thinking about how the needs of a mixed generation congregation and the various church types of worship could be aligned to food. How diverse cultural meals could be analogous with different service styles.

Christmas dinner, delicious, but I wouldn't want one every day or even every week conversely, I enjoy a sandwich on my knee occasionally whilst catching up on a TV programme.

I like a burger, Italian, Indian, Chinese food, not every day but now and then.

My staple diet is fish or chicken with lots of vegetables and / or salad, quite boring to some I'm sure.

However, all this food nourishes and sustains.

Methodist, Baptist, Anglican, Roman Catholic, Free Church, Pentecostal, United Reform, Presbyterian............. Christian teaching from different traditions but all nourishing within foundational parameters of New Testament theology.

We are Christians. Is that not the main thing?

September 1st

The privileges and pit-falls of working with students are well documented. My own relationship with them varies depending on myriad elements around my state on any given day and theirs of course, but we get through and I share their joys and tears throughout their university journeys. I glow with pride when I watch them walk down to their graduations, some with much deserved glory, others by the skin of their teeth.

Today I received a wedding invitation from a student with whom I worked a decade ago and it vindicated all the carrots and sticks I got through with him.

I can't go to the wedding but I wish him every happiness and success and I feel just a little bit chuffed.

September 2nd

Headline:

Future generations of children won't have legs.

Evolutionary changes will already be quietly, subversively getting rid of these unwanted appendages.

No I haven't gone mad. But I am very, very cross.

Every day towns and villages are brought to a standstill, held to ransom by mothers driving their children to school and only a small percentage for whom it is necessary.

It is impossible to get in or out of Cambridge and the villages at school time and, surprising as it may seem, there are other inhabitants who also must use the roads, other members of the community who need to move around.

This is not a 'suffer little children' day.

September 3rd

Ouch, what an old grump I was yesterday.
I won't over-work my frustration, I can't imagine the pressures families live under today, I have no right to be so opinionated, who am I to pass judgment on anybody else's life…..I know I should be breathing deeply, smiling benevolently and exuding patience. I know I should be being saintlier and more 'Christian'.

Best practice is to avoid being on the road at these times or just accept the consequences if there is no alternative, and smile nicely at the neighbouring driver.
Humph!

September 4th

Jesus was asked by the Pharisees when the kingdom of God was coming and he answered:
'The kingdom of God is not coming with things that can be observed…..for in fact the kingdom of God is among you' Luke 17:20
The relevance of this verse is pointing straight at me. What part of the Kingdom was I showing as I gurned and grumbled my way through the traffic the other day? What part of the love of God and neighbour do I reflect as I go to the gym, or to the shops, or anywhere where I don't think I'm being observed?
Note to self: Must do better to live the Kingdom way.

September 5th

Breathe on me Breath of God, fill me with life anew,
That I may love what thou dost love and do what thou wouldst do.

Breathe on me Breath of God until my heart is pure,
Until with thee I will one will to do and to endure.

Breath on me breath of God till I am wholly thine
Until this earthy part of me glows with thy fire divine.

Breathe on me Breath of Go so shall I never die
But live with thee the perfect life of thine eternity.

Edwin Hatch 1835-89.

September 6th

I refuse to let my positive character be undermined by the 'cup-half-empty brigade. There does seem to be quite a lot of them around at the moment. Is it because we are entering autumn after such a lovely summer? Have they got seasonal affected disorder early? Or am I trying to make excuses for their 'Eeyore' dispositions when they've always been like it and I never noticed before? As a spiritual director, I am well trained in listening, in being compassionate and in maintaining a professional yet sympathetic outlook but there are some inveterate moaners with whom I find it hard to be tender.
My father used to say, 'Even heaven will look shabby to folks like that.'
I agree with him.

September 7th

It's late and I should be in bed. I have had a terrific day which started with a ten mile walk along the guided bus way from Histon to St Ives – Cambridgeshire not Cornwall. It isn't particularly scenic, being flat and without any geographical landmarks and it was a grey nothing sort of a morning weather-wise but we have been talking about doing it for a while so realising there was nothing in the diary we decided, over breakfast, to go.

We always have the sort of conversations on long walks that we never have when we're at home. Mainly not about anything earth shattering but just the sort of 'oh by the way' and 'I forgot to tell you' moments that never seem to happen because we aren't often together for extended periods of empty time.

There is a wonderful little café on the High Street at the end of the walk and a toasted teacake and mug of tea never tasted so good.

Carpe Deum. Thank you Lord.

September 8th

One thing that struck me about my 'Examen' last night was simple.

Take time.

Make time.

Yesterday I acknowledged that Peter and I have good conversations and companionable silences when we take ourselves away from our everyday environment just to be together. As someone who has spent time leading Quiet Days and encouraging others to come away to be with God, to leave the everyday stuff behind for a while to be in His company, the parallels were blinding obvious.

A bit more attention to the two of us would be good and needs to happen more often.

September 9th

'Jesus is Lord'
'Whatever you do in word or deed, do all in the name of the Lord Jesus, giving thanks through Him to God the Father.'   Col. 3:17
Lord help me to walk in your way today, to treat everyone I meet with your smile, everyone I touch, touch with your hands.

September 10th

Hildegard of Bingen Day.
What a woman. The more I read of the early female saints the more inadequate I realise my own commitment to faith is.
In 1106 Hildegard was handed into the cloistered life at the age of eight because from the age of three she had been having 'visions' and her parents felt her extraordinary gifts should be given to God to develop. Apart from being a quick pupil in reading and writing she possessed musical awareness and a spirituality which was inexplicable in one so young. She rose through the convent to become the Abbess having suffered many setbacks and much illness, always at its most mortally threatening when she was unable to carry out the various tasks she felt had been given directly by the Holy Spirit. She posed a great threat to the established order of the church, her illnesses usually coming when it had defied or denied her permissions and accesses as she felt she was being led.
Her canon of work which we enjoy today, music, literature and drama has survived because of its academic credibility, compositional integrity and relevance.
To confirm her place in our contemporary world on 7 October 2012 Pope Benedict named her a Doctor of the Church.

September 11th

Another favourite teacher for me is Mother Julian of Norwich.

Very little is known about Julian's life prior to her going into a life of prayer and hermitude. The name 'Julian' is generally thought to have been derived from the Church of St Julian in Norwich, to which her anchorite's cell was joined.

When she was 30 and living at home, Julian suffered from a serious illness. Since she was presumed to be near death, her curate came to administer the last rites of the Catholic Church on 8 May 1373. As part of the ritual, he held a crucifix in the air above the foot of her bed. Julian reported that she was losing her sight and felt physically numb, but as she gazed on the crucifix she saw the figure of Jesus begin to bleed. Over the next several hours, she had a series of sixteen visions of Jesus Christ, which ended by the time she recovered from her illness on 13 May 1373. Julian wrote about her visions immediately after they had happened (although the text may not have been finished for some years) in a version of the Revelations of Divine Love.

Once well again she became an anchorite at the church and convent of St Julian where she remained until her death. The many visitations of the Holy Spirit to her were carefully recorded and even today have wisdom, erudition and teaching for mankind.

The world would do well to go back to a few first principles for rules of life from these early mystics, simplicity, honesty, service and devotion to others just for a start.

September 12th

'Open Houses'
An excuse to do some baking!
I could do lots more but then we would eat it and because we have little or
no self-control when there is cake in the tin, and because a lovely sponge
should be eaten fresh…………!

Anyway a few of us are going to have a fund-raising day, starting with
morning coffee, then lunch and finally afternoon tea. It's ambitious and has
taken a lot of prayerful stepping out in faith but we are opening our homes,
one for each event and hoping for a roaring success.
So, I can bake to my heart's content for the first and last sessions and
indulge in my passion for making soup for the lunchtime sitting, which will
be with me. One of the other girls is a fantastic bread maker so she will be
providing the rolls and loaves to go with it. She too is pleased to have an
excuse to bake saying that the temptation of freshly baked bread in the
house is just too much to resist. Oh yes, I'm with her there.

The fourth member of the team neither bakes nor cooks but is a dab hand
at admin and IT so has taken on the advertising fliers and tickets.

Lead us Heavenly Father Lead us!

September 13th

One more thing about our day, we have decided that we are not going to have endless meetings. We will pray for the project every morning from our own homes but other than an emergency, just quietly, trustfully go about our assigned roles until the final evening before the day.....in two weeks' time.

Thank you Father for the generous invitation I had to be a part of this. Bless us all as we now plan our recipes and start to gather the ingredients together, ultimately to your praise and glory.

September 14th

'There is one body, but it has many parts. But all its many parts make up one body. It is the same with Christ. We were all baptized by one Holy Spirit. And so we are formed into one body. It didn't matter whether we were Jews or Gentiles, slaves or free people. We were all given the same Spirit to drink. So the body is not made up of just one part. It has many parts.

Suppose the foot says, 'I am not a hand, so I don't belong to the body.' By saying this, it cannot stop being part of the body. And suppose the ear says, 'I am not an eye so I don't belong to the body.' By saying this, it cannot stop being part of the body. If the whole body were an eye, how could it hear? If the whole body were an ear, how could it smell? God has placed each part in the body just as he wanted it to be. You are the body of Christ. Each one of you is a part of it.'   1 Corinthians 12: 12-27

That is how feel about being a part of 'Open House'.

September 15th

In the meantime, I must come back into today and as I had a time of quiet this morning thinking particularly about a very sick colleague, I was struck by how very useless I feel. I don't know her well enough to intrude on the family time, I've sent her a card, I have prayed that the Lord will meet them all at their individual points of need but to now walk away and let them get on with it seems quite cold.

We can't be all things to all people. As mothers, I guess we always have an overriding desire to be able to make everything better again.

Holy Mary Mother of God, after what you had to walk away from, help me to put things into perspective, to address any arrogance which makes me think I have anything to offer that Jesus hasn't already got covered.

Amen

September 16th

I was spoken to at the post office this morning by a chap in the queue behind me.

'We're coming to yours next week' he said and a bit preoccupied I said 'Oh are you, that's nice, when?' 'For our lunch, look there on that sign, we've already got our tickets, looking forward to it.' There was a small A5 flier advertising 'Open Houses' pinned in amongst the ads for cleaners, gardeners and dog sitters, I hadn't noticed it.

I asked him his name and who he would be coming with but he must have been a bit deaf because he answered 'Soup, we love soup, it will be homemade won't it?'

'Yes, it will and I look forward to seeing you' I replied.

Once at the counter I asked who he was but they didn't know. How many loose ends there were.

I didn't know him but he clearly knew me. The post office staff didn't know him but he was clearly from the village. One of the others obviously knows him and how lovely that he is looking forward to coming. I must remember to remember him.

September 17th

'The Lord is my light and my salvation', we say it and sing it one way or another every Sunday so that's a lot of repeats across my life. Why then do I STILL need reminding of it?

I am stubborn and stupid that's why.

September 18th

Oh joy, another 'Life-style' leaflet through the door.
Headline:
> **'Thirty pages of great ideas to transform your spare time.'**

If I didn't have to deal with all this tosh I might have some spare time. What spare time anyway? Lord this makes me so crabby. Who are these 'specialists' in life-styles? Wouldn't they be better employed getting out amongst people instead of sitting at their computers thinking up ways to reinvent the wheel?

Spare time I treasure and I have myriad ways of appreciating it when it comes.

September 19th

No 'spare' time today but the promise of deep peace with a prayer workshop, which it is a great privilege to be leading.

Move together individually ……….
>   move into stillness

Move to stop and exclude…………
>   all impediment to sense of self

In the sense of self move towards your soul……….
>   and in the soul of self, see God

Move through stillness into God ……….
>   move into the sweet paradise, which is His stillness

And in that paradise……………………
>   find peace

Be still in that peace ……….
>   and feel the love of God enfold you.

September 20th

Glorious day yesterday and equilibrium restored. Prayer certainly changes things.

We have had a large, late crop of greenhouse tomatoes donated towards our project so today is mapped out as I get these gorgeous red fruits skinned and souped.

Thank you Lord for generous people, help me to recognise and appreciate them more.

Update before bed – I made 4 litres of soup, delicious even if I do say so myself.

September 21st

I am so fired up by getting the cooking off the ground for our special day that I am going to start some baking today for the freezer. I'm using an old Amish cookery book reprint that I bought in Canada whilst visiting my sister. Every page is decorated with beautiful pen and ink drawings of Amish life and the recipes are followed with bible verses which praise and affirm the holiness of domesticity and the grace of home-making.

It is quaintly old fashioned and certainly not PC in these days of 'equality' but there is a purity of purpose about it which celebrates the security that home and food can bring. It affirms unashamedly, the value of making sure the family and community are all nurtured and shown God's love for them through sharing a meal and time round the table.

And isn't that just what we are trying to do in 'Open Houses'?

September 22nd

Loving Lord my bible notes remain unopened on my knee.
I am enthralled and transfixed by the angle of the early morning sun through the tree outside my window. This special time, which I have with you every day has somehow been overridden. The pure light is setting every autumn leaf on fire, orange, red, ochre and still bright green, yellow, maroon, scarlet and claret, merging in to a mirage of unspeakable beauty.
I don't need words today to learn more of you, I don't need my bible to hear you, but thank you for my eyes.
I am seeing your hand in breath-taking majesty and feel very humble and very small and truly awestruck at your greatness.

September 23rd

More baking, poor Peter is being tempted and teased by the wonderful aromas throughout the house but nothing for him. He has observed that the freezer is getting all the love.
Perhaps I should make an extra little something today, especially as we are going to need table erectors and furniture movers in a couple of days' time. I know the chaps have been comparing notes about how very unfair and hard-done-by they all are, I also know that they are totally supportive of what we are doing, they just need a moan, don't we all from time to time.
'Leave all your worries with Him because He cares for you.'   1 Peter 5: 7

September 24th

The girls and I are meeting for a prayer time today to focus on our project and to wait on the Lord for affirmation, guidance and peace. We have each prayed individually over our preparations but a time of collective, quiet reflection away from our kitchens will be special.

Thank you to our elderly neighbour who has offered us her sitting room as a meeting place away from the distractions of our houses. She made the offer some time ago and at the time we hadn't really thought about the need to go somewhere else to meet for prayer but dear Anthea was wise and knew the value and benefit of a safe place, not involved in personal domestic surroundings.

Angels are everywhere.

September 25th

Soup making again today, leek and potato mainly and again all from donated veggies. Once that is simmering I have to step back from 'Open Houses' and meet someone for spiritual direction.

It's always a privilege to walk alongside a directee as they explore and develop their faith and to share some of the burdens that are weighing them down and blocking their receptivity to growth or to celebrate with them over a discovery.

My prayer is that I will be able to focus on them and not let my mind drift back to soup, cake and tablecloths. I'm not being glib, there is huge self-discipline needed to stay in the moment with a directee when one's own life is busy.

Make me a channel of your peace Lord, I pray.

September 26th

Tables and chairs day. Logistics, cups, mugs, bowls and spoons, plates for cake and plates for bread. Knives for butter and knives for cake cutting. Tubs of butter and jars of jam, thank you again for such generous donations, it's the loaves and fishes! There is more than we will ever need I'm sure.

'And my God will supply all your needs according to His glorious riches in Christ Jesus. To our God and Father be glory forever and ever. Amen'
Phil. 4: 19

September 27th

'Open Houses' Day.

11 pm.

I am crying tired tears of unspeakable joy, gratefulness, euphoria and HUGE relief.

32 came for coffee, 25 for lunch and 29 for afternoon tea.

My ears are still ringing with the sound of laughter, words of praise and encouragement. My mind is full of pictures of happy groups enjoying time together round pretty tables or at the sink washing up – who knew how many tea-towels we would need? Clearly twice as many as we had.

There were people from all parts of our lives, around the village, our various clubs and societies and a few friends who had driven over from my previous village. Many we knew but many we met for the first time. Frank and his wife Jill came for lunch, I did recognise him and now I have a name to add to my 'post office' man though I didn't find out how he knew me.

Furthermore, we have £646 to share between our charities.

Steadfast and ever faithful Father God, today you have blessed us as we tried to bless others, Your Holy Spirit has fed us as we fed others. Thank you Lord.

September 28th

'We praise God not to celebrate our own faith but to give thanks for the faith God has in us.'
A line from a wonderfully inspiring book 'Amazing Grace' by an American third order Benedictine Kathleen Norris.
The faith God had in us friends and neighbours to achieve what we did yesterday calls me personally to praise and celebrate the gift that faith in each one of us. I know we could have gone it alone and still been successful in earthly terms but doing it enfolded in faithful love was deeply rewarding and has enriched, not only us but so many of our guests as well.

September 29th

The low after the high; albeit a bit sooner than I might have expected, but the stupefying unkindness of a miserable minority who feel that they were deliberately excluded from being invited to take part in our lovely day is truly hurtful. I see the hand of a jealous malevolence at work trying to spoil any blessed assurance.
It will take time and effort to make a few visits, it will take prayer and patience to try and smooth ruffled feathers but I know that we were transparent from the outset about what we hoped for and to accomplish, and many people made their contributions with open hearts and generosity.
We are in no doubt that we did have the 'Blessed Assurance' of Jesus and that He will now walk with me to be the balm for peace, though it might take time.

September 30th

It is officially autumn judging by the change outside. All my beautiful leaves are being chewed up and spewed out on the fierce gusts of wind which is barrelling around the front of the house.

'The wind blows where it wishes, and you hear its sound, but you do not know where it comes from or where it goes. So it is with everyone who is born of the Spirit.' John 3: 8

We often pray the words, 'in the power of the Spirit' but how would we react if we really witnessed that power coming from us?

October 1st

'It gets earlier every year!'

Christmas music in the shopping precinct. I know I'm old because I'm saying things that only old people say. Perhaps it has something to do with not wishing one's life away. However, I don't know that even as a busy young mum with three small children and a generally hectic life style I would have been in the market for being reminded of Christmas at the beginning of October. They've only just gone back to school for goodness sake.

Now, if I were to get all sanctimonious and ridiculously preachy I could celebrate the fact of the Christmas message being pedalled out loud, to unsuspecting shoppers as early as this. In fact, why not go the whole hog and suggest we keep it mixed in with the rest of the 'musak' constantly blaring out, all year round?

Because, that's why, because; just as we wouldn't have a celebration every day for the other great milestones of life, birthdays, wedding anniversaries etc. some things are so special that we treasure their remembrance and elevate them beyond the 'everyday' on the appropriate date.

So it is with Christmas and this is too early to start.

October 2nd

Does being a Christian full of zeal make one a zealot?

There are some harsh conceptions of a zealot as someone being an uncompromising fanatic.

St Benedict identified two types of zeal; one which leads to bitter division, separating man from God in the pursuit of self-orientated opinion or one which leads man into God and to everlasting life.

Zealot and fundamentalist are two words which have become loaded with aggression and turned from emotions for good into emotions on the edge of reason and thus reasonable behaviour.

To make this vocabulary into wholesome, powerful dialogue we must consistently use it through the application of the Gospel message. That is, that all we do must be in love, in consideration, in selfless service to and of others and in that definition, I'm happy to be a zealot for Christ.

October 3rd

Polarisation is something I understand less and less. I am increasingly compromised in making decisions, no longer seeing things in black and white, more usually seeing everyone's point of view. Am I getting dithery or just mellow? Does my increasing lack of heated involvement mean I no longer care? Is my retreat into prayer a cop-out?

Christ is the fulcrum of my being and so in the gains and losses of this debate or that, this argument or the other, to take myself back into the middle of the field and find the balance is surely an OK place for me to go.

October 4th

'You therefore, beloved, knowing this beforehand, take care that you are not carried away with the error of lawless people and lose your own stability.'

2 Peter 3: 17

Amen.

October 5th

We are going to take the caravan away for half term with our grandchildren. It always involves quite a lot of 'unallowed' behaviour like eating with your fingers - how else should you eat fish and chips? Later bed times - in the hope of later wake up times, some chance! Just hands, face and teeth instead of a shower at bedtime. Chocolate and ice cream on a regular basis. Snuggling up on our bed to watch a film - with popcorn of course, makes for happy little people if a bit gritty in my bed! Lots of made up adventure stories, for which I seem to have gained a reputation, always featuring the appropriately named heroes and heroines.

The company of children is a great learning experience.   Seeing the whole world through their eyes isn't always as simplistic as one might think

October 6th

When the world news is so unremittingly gloomy it is hard to remain optimistic. It has always been our practice to have the news on whilst we have breakfast but some days it really doesn't bode well for the rest of the day. I don't want to live in a 'Pollyanna' world but the grind of demoralising headlines from across the country, across the world is such a psychological barrier to any optimistic outlook, one wonders why it's worth even trying to carry on.

There isn't an option of course, we do carry on, all I am certain of is that without faith it's hard to know how anyone does find a 'raison d'etre'.

I can go back to my 'fulcrum' and my trust in the omnipotent assayer.

October 7th

'Do not use dishonest standards when measuring length, weight or quantity.
Use honest scales and honest weights, an honest ephah and hin.
I am the Lord your God, who brought you out of Egypt.
Keep all my decrees and all my laws and follow them. I am the Lord.'

Lev. 19: 3-6

The holiness of God, the main message of Leviticus is worth revisiting, to relearn the basic tenants of repentance and obedience, of sacrificial redemption, not for Christians through bulls or goats but through Jesus, the Lamb of God.

Knowing where the ultimate power lies in the grand balance of things is always reassuring.

October 8th

Cambridge is restored.

The students are back, term has begun. There's a good chance I'll yet get knocked down by a bike but for the last 800 years town and gown have had an uneasy truce over the common parts and shared spaces. It seems somehow less compatible sharing with tourists over the long summer months even though their spending is a considerable contribution to the city's income.

Anyway, we can now champion the wonders of living in one of the world's finest university cities, trumpet the wealth of cultural opportunities across the artistic spectrum, whilst grousing about youths on bikes thoughtlessly oblivious to pedestrians.

October 9th

I have just finished reading a lovely book called 'The Quaker Café' by Brenda Bevan. The story line was compelling, the writing descriptive without being over intrusive in the story telling and above all it was a testament to the Quaker spirit. I learned a lot about the inner workings of this quiet religious body and feel very drawn to much of their teaching.

I have long championed 'sitting in the presence' to wait on God and how there is no mandate for anyone to have to fill the silence unless truly inspired to and not just because they aren't comfortable with it. The Quaker service is founded on this principle. I also learned a wonderful phrase 'walk in the light'. This commitment to always acknowledge the Lord's presence in such gentle terms, when seeking his guidance to know that the ultimate solution, will be 'to walk in the light' seems so blessedly simple. I know I haven't even scratched the surface but I want to know more.

October 10th

I miss being in a book group. I miss the conviviality of shared conversation, over a glass of wine, enjoying diverse reactions to a text. It always amazed me how many interpretations there were to a given choice and how valid everyone's contribution was to a greater understanding overall.

Therein lies the benefit of a good house group or bible study class; a safe place to discover, unpack and go deeper into passages of scripture; during which fresh perspectives can be introduced and deeper appreciation of the message be absorbed.

That group, I really would miss.

October 11th

We are in our much-loved Northumberland, by a river, on a wonderfully well-run caravan site. We are all set up and the fish and chip van is due within the hour. The family have just texted to say they are about half an hour away and have placed their orders for supper so all we can do now is wait and give thanks for this wonderful opportunity to share a simple few days of fun and relaxation away from rules and timetables. Popcorn and other goodies safely stowed and ready.

I re-read Psalm 138 which I consider our caravan psalm, it begins

'Give thanks to the Lord, for he is good

His love endures forever.'

October 12th

'Be joyful always; pray continually; give thanks in all circumstance, for this is God's will for you in Jesus Christ.'   1 Thess. 5: 18

A busy day, a happy day. Thank you Lord.

October 13th

The plan to stay up later, in order to sleep in, somehow didn't get through to two very excited children who were promised that they could cook their breakfasts on the BBQ with Pops. So, by 7.30 we were prepping and by 8.30 it was all over. Thankfully the river bank provides unlimited entertainment which has the added benefit of little physical input from me other than an ever-watchful eye. So, a couple of happy hours building dams and improving skimming skills, oh and of course getting very wet, passed the majority of the morning very successfully.
Beach this afternoon.

October 14th

Mea culpa, I missed a day's journaling. I only remembered as I was going to sleep but by then was beyond getting back out of bed. I thanked the Lord for another lovely day as I fell headlong into exhausted blackness.

As a Christian, Christ is in me, dwells in me, so he is not a spectator in my life from the outside. My life is from him. That being the case he isn't waiting for me to put on a good show, rather he is the internal fire encouraging me, impelling me, and fuelling me.

Therefore, I think it would have been an empty gesture to get back up out of bed, feeling a bit cross that I hadn't written up the day.

October 15th

It seems a bit arrogant to assume I might know the mind of God!
Just a bit!!
How many times I assume to know what the Lord might say, or think?
On the one hand, we are all encouraged to think of God the Father and through Jesus address him albeit with respect but as Father.
On the other hand, his awesome majesty and being is beyond even the most insightful comprehension.
So, it really is arrogant to assume to know the mind of God and perhaps I should think a little more before saying what *I* think he might think or say.
That all came about because after we had waved the family off we went for a walk and passed a hedgerow of 'fly-tipped' builders rubble which led to anger and despair at the people with whom we share our space. Then onto global issues and before we knew it the whole universe was making God weep or so *I* assumed.

October 16th

A glorious autumn day for our homeward drive and on thinking about our hurt on behalf of God yesterday, we instead made a positive commitment to celebrate the joy of the last few days. To be happy and grateful for the opportunity, our health, and the family, to make good memories and wholesome personalities, which must please God.
There *I* go again.

Oct 17th

Today would have been my deceased sister's birthday. She died with her family, her husband and two little boys, in January 1981 whilst staying in a caravan in Austria on a skiing holiday. A caravan....it was a long time before I came around to having one, that's for sure!
Anyway, the years since she went, don't count. I sometimes feel like I could touch her, that she only just went but at other times it's almost like she was a part of someone else's story. I have things in the kitchen which belonged to her that I use every day, like a large wooden shopping board, and a milk jug which, although precious, I do use. I wonder about her boys who were two and five years old and who, now, would be fine men holding their place in family and community life.
Morning has come from mourning, new days rise and have beauty, somehow deeper and more intense, coloured by an appreciation of life. Coloured by having had such a kind, lovely person for a sister.

October 18th

Saint Ignatius wrote at length about sin. 'General Examination of Conscience' at the beginning of his Spiritual Exercises encourages one to dig deep into one's heart and soul in order to purify the body – the Temple of the Holy Spirit.

He wrote of three kinds of thought; the first, one's own, arising from personal freedom and desire and the other two, one from the good spirit and one from the evil. So, we must then be aware of where a thought has come from and then how we will deal with it.

On EVIL, we must:

Firstly, resist it immediately and thus it is conquered.

The **second** way to 'merit' from an evil thought is, when it reoccurs time after time and one resists continually until it is overcome and goes away. This gains more merit than the easier first option according to Ignatius.

The **third** and more dangerous is when we give heed to a thought which we know to be wrong and yet dwell on it, getting some pernicious pleasure from picking away at it and its consequences.

I have plenty of those and know I dwell for far too long on antagonistic thoughts, compounding the sin to an even greater level. The Spiritual Exercises are a powerful journey of self into prayer and prayerful deliberation on God grace, often taken in a four-week retreat but more practically in shorter week-long sessions. It is a hard walk to make but puts a depth of insight into one's own precious gift of spirituality and union with God.

October 19th

I don't seem to have conquered the third 'thought' clause except that I try to recognise it and nip it in the bud, sometimes more successfully than others.

If I dwell in pensive regret however, I am also sinning in letting sin get the upper hand. Sufficient to confess 'with a contrite heart' and then walk out 'in the light'.

October 20th

May the mind of Christ my Saviour
Live in me from day to day,
By His love and power controlling
All I do or say.
May the word of God dwell richly
In my heart from hour to hour,
So that all may see I triumph
Only through His power.
May the love of Jesus fill me
As the waters fill the sea,
Him exulting, self-abasing
This is victory.

Kate B Wilkinson 1859-1928

October 21st

Although not yet Advent we are starting to look forward in planning terms to church Christmas decorations, advent plays, school concerts and choir performances.

The church is such a fundamental part of community at the great festivals of the year, also the place where Hatch, Match and Dispatch happens. It is a place greedy for funds to keep its perilously fragile edifice in good order, its antiquated heating working, the wheezing bellows of the organ supple.

Are WE not the church? Is that not what we are taught these days? Not the building itself.

The arguments about buildings, holy or otherwise, redundant or otherwise are rumbling ever louder in these times of scarce funding, and perhaps those who are less regular attendees, but who shout the loudest when their place of worship is threatened, might consider putting in a few more appearances a year.

In a State Homily of 1571 it was written

'And to the intent ye may understand further why churches were built, that God might have his place, and that God might have his time duly to be honoured and served of the multitude of the parish……..'.

I rest my case.

October 22nd

My friend Annie has just returned from a Caribbean cruise and I felt quite envious when I saw her relaxed, sun kissed, smiling face. Then of course I was ashamed of myself.

It turns out she had a shocking time with a bad tummy bug in the first few days and a worrying time with hospital visits towards the end trying to diagnose a cardiac arrhythmia. Her hours on deck in the sun were prescriptive because she was too weak to enjoy the other activities and visits in which everyone else was taking part.

So then I was doubly ashamed.

But since the sin of picking over a sin, to feel even worse, is a sin in itself, I'm done with it. I am grateful that my friend is home safely, I love her and will do whatever I can to support her.

October 23rd

Annie said, 'My friends are the 'salt of the earth'.

We have rallied around as she gets hospital appointments and test dates for her cardiac problem which is rather bigger than first imagined, in fact her consultant has expressed surprise that she wasn't flown home from the ship.

'Salt of the earth' is such a warm biblical expression and even in these days of cutting it back out of our diets we still need some and need more than ever, the interpretation from Matthew's Gospel passage.

If seasoning has no flavour it has no value. If Christians make no effort to affect the world around them, what use are they to God's Kingdom?

October 24th

Indispensable as salt is to ourselves, it was even more so to the Hebrews, being to them not only an appetizing condiment in food, but also entering largely into the religious services of the Jews as an accompaniment to the various offerings presented on the altar. Fortunately they possessed an inexhaustible and ready supply of it on the southern shores of the Dead Sea. The salt-pits formed an important source of revenue to the country. Also as one of the most essential articles of diet, salt symbolized hospitality, durability, fidelity and purity, and was valuable as an antiseptic. Hence the Hebrew expression 'covenant of salt', denoting the alliance between friends and again, the expression 'salted with the salt of the palace'. Ezra 4:14, not meaning that they had 'maintenance *from* the palace,' as some would have it, but that they were bound by sacred obligations and fidelity to the king. In the present day, 'to eat bread and salt together' is an expression for a league of mutual amity. It was probably with a view to keep this idea prominently before the minds of the Jews that the use of salt was enjoined on the Israelites in their offerings to God.

October 25th

There seems to have been a theme running the last few days and today was no exception, I was making chutney and piccalilli. So, 'salting down' or preserving, for the larder and Christmas presents. The house still smells of spices and vinegar tonight, I guess it will for a day or two.
Thank you Mother for showing me how to do these things, I know I could look it all up on YouTube but my memories of our seasonal cook-ins are a precious link to you.

October 26th

Talking of Christmas presents I am going into Cambridge, with the express intention of doing some Christmas shopping. I could go on-line and let a courier take the strain out of it all but I enjoy looking, touching, feeling and deliberating, moreover, I don't enjoy having to re-parcel and return things when they aren't quite right. I know it isn't yet November and I know I grumble about Christmas being earlier every year but I feel I want to make a start.

I will go the Fitzwilliam Museum shop and drool over all the beautiful things for sale and convince myself that I'm supporting a worthy cause by shopping there, I might even have some lunch as well.

Lord thank you for this day and for my anticipation, it's good to be alive.

October 27th

Oh dear, the best laid plans of mice and men!

I did go to the museum and then went into the Picture Gallery just to pay homage to the Nicholas Poussin picture 'Extreme Unction' which is quite recently acquired. From its first unveiling I have been drawn to it, not from any morbid obsession with death but for the precision and beauty with which every inch of the canvas is worked. The priestly vestments, the chrism and holy vessels have all been painted with immense sensitivity to their function and the clothing and postures of the family surrounding the death bed are anatomically and gymnastically graceful, their faces suffused with the agony of parting. It is the loveliest depiction of how one might leave this world with dignity and love.

As ever I spent a long time working my way across the canvas, up and down, not wanting to miss a crumb of the content and every time I find something I hadn't notice before.

A good death is surely every human being's desire.

I didn't feel like shopping afterwards.

October 28th

Last week coincided with the very sudden and very sad death of a friend's husband this time last year. Yes, it was a peaceful passing but the shock to the family was too visceral to make the placid letting-go in the Poussin painting anything but a fantasy. Having time and the conscious capacity to receive extreme unction, the last rites or even a prayer, is a gift.
Wasn't it St Augustine who said, 'Lord preserve me from sudden death'?
I guess as a Christian one would hope to be able to make that final journey into the loving arms with some pain free awareness of leaving.

October 29th

Away with the introspection of the last few days!
After some mundane domestics this morning, I had a surprise visit from an old friend visiting the local hospital and who had just popped round 'on spec.' for a cup of coffee. Coffee turned into lunch and at 4pm, realising the time and not wanting to be on the motorway at rush hour she left.
Spontaneity was her gift to me. I'm so glad she called round. It made me feel special that she wanted to share so much of her time with me.
I treasure my friends and am incredibly blessed by their loyalty and love.
Father God thank you for my friends, help me never to underestimate their love for me.

October 30th

Still, deep, quiet, gentle, prayerful, rocking.
Still, deep, quiet, gentle, prayerful.
Still, deep, quiet, gentle.
Still, deep, quiet.
Still, deep.
Still.
So I come.

October 31st

After the picture on a children's Bible:

The Lamb on the shepherd's shoulder
looked so safe and clean,
the shepherd gave his body
on which the Lamb could lean.
The Lamb became the shepherd
in an act of supreme love
and the Lamb then carried the shepherd
with the power of a Dove.
The Dove wrapped wings of Holy strength
over shepherd and his flock and
God was in the bird of light
Messiah over all.

November 1st

Some things just don't translate even in our own language. Family sayings have no direct meaning 'syntaxically' but to other members of the clan are the lingua franca.
I was reminded of this when I was offered a piece of cake yesterday and I without thinking I replied that yes please I would but just 'a scrockit'.
The raised eyebrows of the server made me realise what I'd said I of course apologised and asked for just a small piece.
That's what a 'scrockit' is, it's a small piece, a little taste.

November 2nd

My grandson asked me last night if I was excited now that November is here because it's my birthday soon. Bless him, I said yes of course. I couldn't disappoint that little smiling face full of expectation by saying that I would rather not be having another birthday, that I wanted to stop the clock, that I want to freeze-frame the day, that I want him to stay as gorgeous as he is at the moment, or me as well as I am or Peter as fit as he is or ....
I can no more stop the clock than push back the tide, I can no more save my little people from the hurts of growing up than I can hold myself in this moment of good health. All I can do is be very 'in the moment' to seize a modern idiom. All I can do is live as well, as fully and with as much love as possible every second of every day.
And I know that as my birthday draws near I will get excited because I love surprises and I love getting post.

November 3rd

There was a gift today however, a glorious, hot, sunny day. Just after the weatherman had said about the record hottest day for November being a year ago, we got another one. Not a record breaker but a generous, meteorological gift to lift spirits and perhaps nudge a few folks into feeling glad to be alive.

'Praise the Lord from the heavens
praise him in the heights above.
Praise him, all his angels, all his heavenly hosts.
Praise him sun and moon, praise him
All you shining stars.
Praise the Lord you men and maidens
Old men and children of the earth.
Praise the Lord.'   Condensed from Ps 148

November 4th

'By the Grace of God I am what I am and his Grace bestowed upon me was not (is not) in vain.'

This reading from Corinthians via my on-line daily notes reminds me of so many things. Firstly, how much I value the daily prompting every morning, right there when I log on. I don't need to open a book of either notes or even my bible, it's all there in one email. That makes me sound less than committed but there are days when without this link, I'm not sure I would truthfully, determinedly get around to it. Thank you compilers.

Secondly, this reading I think is telling me that humility is not convincing myself of uselessness and worthlessness but of recognising God's work in me. It is encouraging me to see myself through God's eyes and therefore to acknowledge his ability, his Grace, to bring out the best in me.

Long way to go but I'm not doing it unaided.

179

November 5th

'I couldn't face one day without you by my side.'
'My love's inside you even more than you know.'
'I fight you because I know you'll always love me.'
'I'll never walk alone.'
'I want to hold your hand.'
'I finally found the one'.

These are lines from a few different pop songs on the radio this morning.
Love songs, songs of commitment, Songs of appreciation, of praise?
Hymns, songs, songs, hymns,
Just keep singing.

November 6th

It is so easy to get downhearted and disillusioned about the state of the world and particularly in what I think of as The Holy Land.
There is though, a small group working under the name 'Embrace the Middle East' the former 'Bible Lands' mission, who are bringing real and lasting change to the area through education, healthcare, and community building, development projects. Working particularly in Lebanon, Egypt, the West Bank and Gaza they are running schools for children and hygiene clinics for adults, basic repair and maintenance workshops and back to the land agriculture and farming practice classes.
I know I have been de-sensitised over the years to the ongoing problems of these poor regions but this is really hands on help to promote self-sufficiency and independence and it is so positive.
God never gives up on me so I shouldn't give up on his world.

November 7th

When someone asks you to pray for them what do they expect?
Do they want you to badger God on their behalf? Do they want you to mention them in passing? Do they assume that you will do it with some measure of regularity? Do they believe that the more folks they get 'on-side' the louder the noise will be so God WILL hear? Do they ask you because they think your prayers are better than theirs?
On the other side of this request is the burden being laid on the intercessor. How do you do your best by the request? How should you honour the trust that has been placed in you? With all the other prayer requests you carry, how should you prioritise one from another?
I am asked these questions regularly and I do mean regularly, maybe weekly.
The only way I can answer is to share what I do. I have a small note book in which I always jot down names and situations as they are brought to me and in my quiet time, at some point in the day I hold all that I have written up to God, and pray that he will meet each one at their own personal point of need.
Prayer is a way of us wrapping a blanket of love and support around someone.

November 8th

In the Cathedral

The bell rings and the pilgrims pray, like Pavlov's dogs they respond to clapper on brass. Maybe this enforced moment of quiet repose will imprint deep and lead to a remembrance when away from this place. An instinct fledged in a day out to an historic monument, that when a bell rings their response will be to say 'Our Father'.
They gasp at the beauty of carvings in stone and they marvel at the craft of ages long removed from any comprehension yet contemporary enough to resonate in their finer feeling. Maybe their eyes will be encouraged to consider the indwelling beauty of lives lived outside this holy place but holding the sacredness of God.

November 9th

I recharged my batteries yesterday as I waited in the cathedral to meet my grandsons, it was lovely.
I just sat and looked around me, at things I've seen dozens of times before, yet I always notice something new when I do it.
Does God only reveal himself to me in bite sized pieces I wonder, or am I so superficial that just like skim reading an article, I skim over what I do and don't observe; like listening with half an ear so only getting half a story; like dosing in front of a programme I particularly want to watch.
Dear Lord help me to keep awake to all the possibilities which you constantly present to me.

November 10th

Winter is here. Cold driving rain from a heavy grey sky with no breaks to promise anything is going to improve any time soon.

What have I been putting off doing that I could use today for? Tidying, deep cleaning, Christmas card list, reading, praying; pity that came last, catch-up phone calls.

Father God, thank you for today and that whatever happens I know you are with me, help me not to waste it but to appreciate every moment, even if I am only sitting at my kitchen table with *Another Pot of Coffee*.

November 11th

Yesterday, whilst having that second cup of coffee, the thought came to me, make the Christmas cake!! I was suddenly totally enthused. Wrapped up against the rain I went to our local supermarket to get a few missing items for the recipe and then to the happy task.

Christmas CD playing, I weighed and measured, soaked and steeped so that by lunch time the kitchen was starting to smell lovely. Because I hadn't soaked the fruit overnight in orange juice, I followed a tip from the internet and whizzed it in the microwave for a couple of minutes. The juxtaposition of microwave and my grandmother's 100 year old recipe made me smile.

Early afternoon saw the cake into the oven and from then on for the rest of the day the house smelt wonderfully of the promise of Christmas. No synthetic candle on earth, however expensive can replicate it.

Thank you Lord for hearing my prayer yesterday.

November 12th

'Therefore, since we have a great high priest who has gone through the heavens, Jesus Son of God, let us hold firmly to the faith we profess. For we do not have a high priest who is unable to sympathise with our weaknesses, but we have one who has been tempted in every way, just as we are - yet who is without sin.
Let us then approach the throne of grace with confidence, so that we may receive mercy and find grace to help us our time of need.   Heb. 4: 14-16

November 13th

'Let us hold firmly'.
Loving Lord squash the cynicism, the despondency and doubt which I feel when I let the horrors of the daily news undermine my belief that God *is* greater than mere mortals.

November 14th

'The Lord Bless you and keep you,
The Lord make his face to shine upon you and be gracious towards you,
The Lord turn his face towards you and give you his peace
Today and forever'.   Numbers 6: 24-26
This prayer is printed on a bookmark which a colleague gave me. She isn't a Christian but she thought the words were lovely and thought I would appreciate it.
A little bookmark which, maybe, sowed in her the seeds of knowing, of growing to know God through her kind gesture to me.
It is also my prayer for her.

November 15th

Children in Need week is in full swing. A huge example of the generosity and goodness of spirit which pervades this country. Despite trouble and insurrection all around, the British public rises to the challenge every year with renewed determination to make a real change for the less fortunate.

We might be disentangling from Europe, we might feel like strangers in a foreign land that we once took for granted, but this appeal year in, year out celebrates the profound goodness of the British people across race, creed and gender to make a better world.

November 16th

I have been collecting a little pile of post for a few days now, waiting for this morning to enjoy the thoughtful blessings and birthday wishes from my friends and family.

It is beyond my comprehension that many people won't get a card, haven't got anyone to remember them, or just say 'Happy Birthday' to them. I know they are out there but not who they are, otherwise I could remember them. I think I know my neighbours, but do I?

November 17th

One great project every year at this time is the 'Shoe Box' collection.

Since 1990, more than 124 million boys and girls in over 150 countries have experienced God's love through the power of simple shoebox gifts from Operation Christmas Child.

Together with thousands of volunteers around the UK, we are able to share the love of Jesus Christ and the joy of Christmas with millions of children.

There is so much love in each box that the misery inflicted by corrupt individuals, war or famine is wiped away and goodness prevails for a brief moment in these precious lives.

November 18th

I've been had again! Or so it would seem.

Almost weekly I get a bag through the door asking for any unwanted clothes for one worthy cause or another. Usually I take my things to the charity shop in the village but on this occasion and because it was a cause I felt I trusted asking for help, I had a little clear-out.

Now I find out that it was a scam as were so many of the collections this past year and that an unscrupulous gang drive the streets picking up the bags very early on collection day. That means that the honest collectors miss out in their donations.

Two days' diary, two different attitudes. I should wonder about these people and pray for them - somehow!

November 19th

It's fashionable to knock simple thoughts, free from academic conceits and literary constructs but the poems of Ella Wheeler Wilcox speak volumes in their honesty.

Don't look for the flaws as you go through life;
And even when you find them,
It is wise and kind to be somewhat blind
And look for the virtue behind them.
For the cloudiest night has a hint of light
Somewhere in its shadows hiding;
It is better by far to hunt for a star,
Than the spots on the sun abiding.

The current of life runs ever away
To the bosom of God's great ocean.
Don't set your force 'gainst the river's course
And think to alter its motion.
Don't waste a curse on the universe –
Remember it lived before you.
Don't butt at the storm with your puny form,
But bend and let it go o'er you.

The world will never adjust itself
To suit your whims to the letter.
Some things must go wrong your whole life long,
And the sooner you know it the better.
It is folly to fight with the Infinite,
And go under at last in the wrestle;
The wiser man shapes into God's plan
As water shapes into a vessel.

Ella Wheeler Wilcox

Reproduced by kind permission of the Ella Wheeler Wilcox Society, USA

November 20th

'As water shapes into a vessel'

Lord shape me according to *your* plan, not to my whim.

Amen.

November 21st

Running away to 'the bosom of God's ocean' sounds a bit scary because I'm not a good swimmer and certainly I would hate to be adrift on a great big open sea. I can't make anything good from that thought apart from the fact that I would have to be 200% relying on his grace to keep me from harm.
Maybe it serves to remind me that God isn't just a warm fleecy blanket but that I am answerable for my actions for good or ill and that I will have a case to answer in the final analysis.

November 22nd

The General Confession at the beginning of Morning Prayer in The Book of Common Prayer begins:
'Almighty and most merciful Father, we have erred and strayed from thy ways like lost sheep. We have followed too much the devices and desires of our own hearts'.
The gravity and the beauty of the words inspire one to a heartfelt apology than rather than the watered-down version we use now and I if wonder if it would be such a bad thing for there to be a little bit more respectful language in some of our prayers.
I don't want to be chummy and pals with my Father God, just loving and respectful of a generous, hugely wise God the Father.

November 23rd

I seem to have had few days of quite deep thinking and remember that it often strikes me like this before advent, more so than Lent strangely. There is so much excitement and commercial hysteria building and we aren't even at December yet, I feel a bit Bah Humbug about it.
A performance of the Messiah this weekend will put me back in a rightful mind I know.
'Rejoice, Rejoice greatly, oh daughter of Zion;'
'Behold I tell you a mystery;'
Hallelujah the Lord omnipotent reigneth and other glorious parts.'
will do the job wonderfully.

November 24th

'Rejoice in the Lord always, I will say it again: Rejoice. Let your gentleness be evident to all. The Lord is near. Do not be anxious about anything but in everything, by prayer and petition, with thanksgiving, present your requests to God'.   Phil. 4: 4-6
Then what?
'And the peace of God, which transcends all understanding, will guard your mind and heart.'   Verse 7
That's what!

189

November 25th

That peace, which we know the world cannot give, doesn't come from mindfulness or living in the moment. It doesn't come from positive thinking or good vibes. It comes from knowing that God is in control, it comes from believing, even when it's hard to believe, that God is in control. It is found in the quiet of deep prayer, of prayer given the time and space to develop and water the anxious places.

God always has time for us, I should make more time to be with him.

November 26th

When I'm Queen!

Only my friends will get driving licences, that will mean only people with manners.

Only those known to me personally will be allowed to sit near me in the cinema - that will mean no one with a bucket of popcorn or a gallon cup of something to slurp.

Only those who can walk in a straight line and with a determined gait, which means no one wandering aimlessly, drifting from side to side, cluttering up the pavement, can be out shopping with me.

I thought I was reasonable?

November 27th

Yesterday's murmurings came after an hilarious coffee time with my daughter and her friends who started to moan about things that annoyed them. 'When I'm Queen' escalated into a really good verbal clearing out of the grudges and gripes about our fellow citizens, not many of which were altogether PC but mostly great fun.

As I drove home I was still thinking about it.

Then this morning, as I had to leap into the road to avoid a mother pushing a pram the size of a Sherman tank and her other child on its scooter, I realised I haven't even scratched the surface of my 'When I'm Queen' thoughts.

November 28th

Sometimes finding the right card is impossible, even though there are more card shops on the High Street than ever. I want one for my son-in-law. I can find funny, silly ones, I can find gushing 'not my style' ones but not one which says:

'Thank you for being an incredible husband to my daughter and wonderful father to my grandsons. Thank you for becoming such a precious addition to our family and accepting us warts and all. For your humour, caring, and genuine warmth, thank you.

So, it's a blank, hand written one, which perhaps, is actually far more sincere.

I hope so.

November 29th

It's a very cold, raw day and I can't seem to concentrate on anything, what am I brewing?

My Aunt used to use that expression, 'You look hot' she'd say, 'What are you brewing?'

Tea gets brewed, beer gets brewed.

As a child with a fertile imagination I loved my 'Illustrated Junior Shakespeare' and I enjoyed looking at the picture of the Witches from Macbeth, round the cauldron brewing:

'Fillet of a fenny snake, in the cauldron boil and bake;

Eye of newt, and toe of frog, wool of bat, and tongue of dog,

Adder's fork, and blind-worm's sting, lizard's leg, and howlet's wing,

For a charm of powerful trouble, like a hell-broth boil and bubble.'

I'm not sure I feel that bad.

November 30th

Stinking cold, that's what I was 'brewing' and it has come out in full today. Eyes and nose running, sore throat and clogged up ears. I am going to cancel going to a meeting, which is unheard of but I should not be sharing this with anyone else, and anyway I just want to stay on the sofa in front of the fire and moan at the rubbish on daytime television.

December 1st

St Andrew's Day

The New Testament states that Andrew was the brother of Simon Peter so a son of John, or Jonah. He was born in the village of Bethsaida on the Sea of Galilee. Both he and his brother Peter were fishermen by trade, hence the tradition that Jesus called them to be his disciples by saying that he will make them 'fishers of men'.

In the Gospel of Matthew (Matt 4:18-22) and in the Gospel of Mark (Mark 1:16-20) Simon Peter and Andrew were both called together to become disciples of Jesus and 'fishers of men'. These narratives record that Jesus was walking along the shore of the Sea of Galilee, observed Simon and Andrew fishing, and called them to follow him.

How especially different must Jesus have been, that two hardened fishermen would just down tools and follow him because he asked them to. I cannot conceive of a situation where I would just up and go because someone walked onto my patch and said 'Follow me'.

December 2nd

Still alive, just; but pleasure yesterday to watch the original 1961 West Side Story film with George Chakiris and Natalie Wood, from my bed of suffering.

Clearly, if one searches there *is* good viewing during the day and I was making stereotypically rash generalisations without really knowing.

I'm sorry. Do I do it a lot, I wonder, and haven't noticed? – Yes I do!

Time to take stock.

December 3rd

I have turned a corner, I will live. Apart from the unattractive scabs and abrasions around my nose and top lip there is little evidence of the very parlous state that was my health for the past few days.

I know I take my health for granted and it's only when I am the slightest bit under the weather that I ever stop to think about those suffering every minute of every day with chronic discomfort. They are saints and they deserve the right to be irritable and short tempered with the rest of us. They, however, are usually the ones who have somewhere, somehow reached a quietude in their suffering which makes me moaning about a cold seem puerile and downright stupid.

Father God again I ask you to forgive me and show me how to live in grace, whatever my circumstances.

December 4th

As if to waken me up from my pathetic, complacent torpor after a bad cold, the sight of the flooded homes in the Lake District and North Yorkshire; of Christmas decorations sodden and ruined, floating in a sea of detritus, thrown out of the spoiled houses, is truly awful. People's lovingly wrapped presents reduced to bloated masses of papier-mâché; the frail and elderly, nursing mothers and their children, loved dogs and cats, all being boated away from their houses, their places of refuge and safety – not knowing when or even if they will be able to return, all this misery is too painful to watch from the comfort of a warm dry home.

Where will they go, what will they do? I feel so guilty at being safe and in awe of the workforce rescuing, helping and supporting these communities.

Don't let this just be another news item to me, what can I do?

December 5th

The local Salvation Army have posted on the village web page what and when they are collecting, so something concrete to be able to do, clothes for all ages and Christmas presents for the children are at the top of the list. Apparently major haulage and building merchants across the country are wading in, literally, to support the aid organisations. We do have an amazing esprit de corps in this country, underneath the national moaning pessimism, which is sometimes so warping.

The local Hindu Gurdwara has set up a relay of feeding kitchens to ensure hot food is available to the workers and dispossessed and the Mosque has made an open house place of refuge day and night.

Faith in action, truly.

December 6th

Fighting the elements
Fighting the men in suits
Fighting for basic needs
Should a fight be necessary?
Begging hands hold cracked old bowl
Begging eyes show empty soul
Begging just for basic needs
Should begging be necessary?
Here the floods with too much water
There the desiccated earth
Narratives of supply and need
Highlighted at this time of
Annual greed and frenzy.
Is equilibrium attainable at all?
Is equilibrium achievable for all?
Is equilibrium necessary?

December 7th

Its late, 11pm.

I have been at an Advent Retreat day today and feel quite stirred up by it.

Not the peacefulness I had hoped for nor the quiet heart I had expected. I think I am too preoccupied with the world, with things way outside my remit or control. I enjoyed the choice of readings and reflections and entered the quiet times with open expectation of finding space for meditation on things designed to centre my trust and faith. Even the silent, shared lunch taken to a rendition of Gregorian chants was beautifully, serenely engineered.

Why then have I not been able to step away from the agitation I feel inside?

I think my disappointment is a lesson to me, reminding me of the bafflement that lots of people of faith feel when their expectations of God are not met in the way they wanted or hoped for, and it hurts.

Father God thank you for today and for the leaders and the love they put into the programme. Thank you for showing me that although not meeting my expectations you have more than met me at my point of need and again taught me a valuable lesson.

December 8th

What a great family service today followed by the parish bring and share lunch. It was a celebration of family, of community, of belonging and everyone who had brought a neighbour, not someone from church, to join in, was touched at the welcome extended to them.

Lord what a privilege it is to relax into your generous embrace, to 'Let go and Let God' as the poster outside the Baptist Church says.

It sounds trite but I maybe I should line it up for my New Year resolution.

Let Go and Let God.

December 9th

I saw a procession of children from a primary school this morning, many of them dressed up for a nativity play which was lovely. There were lots of shepherds and wise men, lots of angels and 'Mary's helpers'. There were also children in national costumes from around the world. Surely only through children growing up learning about other faiths and cultures can we ever hope for a more tolerant and peaceful world.
'And a little child shall lead them', and show how respect, friendship and understanding blots out fear and division.
Lord can we hope to learn from them.

December 10th

'Oh Ma, you are so sweet!' was the reaction of my daughter when I shared yesterday's thought with her.
She pointed out to me that the innocence of children could never be carried through to adulthood because we need suspicion and an awareness of danger to survive and they come from learning to mistrust, not trust.
And a little child shall lead them? And my child is still leading me I suppose.
Maybe I could just pray that 'purity of consideration' be a trait worth fostering because that covers all the bases I think and translates from the playground into adult life.

December 11th

We are off to Newcastle to do the 'sleigh run'. To our son and his family. The weather forecast isn't particularly good for the north east but when is it ever at this time of year? We've got plenty of clothing contingenties in the car so we will be fine whatever arrives.

Last year at much the same time, we all went off to buy their Christmas tree as the snow began to fall and there was enough on the ground when we got back to build a modest snowman and throw a few snowballs at each other. Of course, it all got a bit macho between our son, his son and Pops and we all ended up very cold and wet but the joy and delight on the faces of the children at seeing the grown-ups behaving so playfully was fabulous. Hot chocolate with marshmallows followed, round the fire, and another happy memory was created.

December 12th

I felt ready this morning to be swept up in the excitement of Christmas. I love the old, rather hackneyed songs and have to restrain myself from singing along when I'm in the shops where they are being played.

Today in the precinct I heard the song 'Silver Bells' a good oldie by Jay Livingstone and Ray Evans, the lines:

'City sidewalks, busy sidewalks dressed in holiday style
Children laughing, people passing, meeting smile after smile'

I bounced out into the street to be confronted by a rough sleeper. How near the surface my emotions are? My bubble was burst and I was then cross that I had had to come face to face with the reality of a lot of people's lives in the midst of my own warm cocoon.

I salved my conscience, bought some food and took it back to the man and said a prayer for the Street Pastors who are out seven nights a week looking after the homeless.

So little, and I still feel useless.

December 13th

The last of a series of meetings before the break and I held fast to Proverbs 15:1
'A gentle answer turns away wrath but a harsh word stirs up anger.'
I needed to keep saying it to myself in my head and thank the Lord for it, because a bridge was built for us to proceed into a new year on a much surer footing.
And talking of sure footings it's our wedding anniversary, which after 48 years must mean we are on fairly safe ground.

December 14th

'Better a meal of vegetables where there is love,
than a fattened calf with hatred.'
Another proverb, very current for today and one I should have writ large on the wall above my cooker, since I seem to have to cook for vegetarians, pescatarians, vegans, myriad allergies and digestive disturbances.
The irony of all these intolerances, medical or moral, in a world of hunger, is unsettling.

December 15th

My Hope is built on nothing less
Than Jesus' blood and righteousness
No merit of my own I claim
But wholly trust in Jesus' name.
On Christ the solid rock I stand
All other ground is sinking sand.

Amen

Edward Mote 1797 - 1874

December 16th

It's my daughter's birthday today but she doesn't want a fuss so we aren't going to make one.........
Just a cake and presents and supper with the family. No fuss for such a special person, I don't think anyone was going to let that happen!
Thank you for all you are to so many people special daughter, loving wife, lovely Mum, great sister, trustworthy and loyal friend and great cake maker.
Also, now your birthday has happened, perhaps we can start decorating for Christmas?

December 17th

Overflowing love is the natural response to forgiveness and as surely as I realise the sin in me and the need for forgiveness, so I recognise the completeness of God's forgiveness to me.
The cleansing relief of making my confession before receiving the sacrament of the Eucharist, and believing in absolution from God, is wonderful.
Lord accept my love I pray.

December 18th

With the daily arrival of so many good wishes on big cards, little cards and now E cards, we are reminded of all the friends we have around the world and although for many it is only this annual ritual that keeps us in touch, keep us in touch it does.
Ralph Waldo Emerson said:
'The glory of friendship is not the outstretched hand, not the kindly smile, not the joy of companionship; it is the spiritual inspiration that comes to one when you discover that someone else believes in you and is willing to trust you with a friendship.'

December 19th

More cards, more lovely letters of friendship.

'Time does not take away from friendship, not does separation.' Tennessee Williams said, and for all my bookworm buddies, PG Wodehouse wrote:

'There is no surer foundation for a beautiful friendship than a mutual respect for literature.' The Bard himself wrote: 'Words are easy like the wind, faithful friends are hard to find.'

Going back further, Cicero observed that: 'Friendship improves happiness and abates misery by doubling our joys and dividing our grief.'

Lastly for my dear, precious girlfriends, you know who you are; the witty observer Dorothy Parker wrote: 'Constant use had not worn ragged the fabric of their friendship.'

There is nothing ripped, ragged or frayed about the love I have for you, it is whole and strong and beautiful.

December 20th

Hair, nails and feet today ready for the big festival, Christmas holidays.

Not just 'The Holidays' as they are known in the United States but The Christmas Break or the Christmas Holidays.

This is not just any holiday, not to me and just as I happily wish my Muslim friends Happy Eid at the end of Ramadan, my Jewish friends Happy Hanukah, or my Hindu colleagues Happy Diwali, so I expect to be offered 'Christmas' wishes.   I   also   expect   the   freedom   to   make   that acknowledgement to others without having to be apologetic about it.

So, today is self-indulgent pampering for me and I am going to enjoy it, my present to me before I finish off the trimmings around the house.

December 21st

Whilst I was being fussed over yesterday I found myself thinking about the last few days writing about friendship and, suddenly, I wanted to cry because I started to remember the lonely people who, at this time of year seem sadder and more disenfranchised than ever. Those for whom there is no point in getting their hair done or having their nails polished, those who have no one to make festive food and special treats for. We, like most other church communities are trying to make sure that there is no one in our individual vicinity needing company. We have all been asked to take the streets immediately round our homes and to account for all our neighbours. There will be those who don't want to be bothered or included in any initiatives and we must respect them but please Lord lead us, lead me, to anyone who would relish some company in a family home for a few hours.

December 22nd

Dear Holy Mary, Mother of God,

My thoughts and prayers are for you today. As your time approaches, however many millennia have passed, Christian mothers around the globe remember the apprehension of their delivery date. They remember the last-minute shopping, the last-minute cleaning, the last-minute checking of their hospital bag and of the newly decorated nursery waiting for the little bundle.

What you had, or didn't have is beyond modern women's comprehension. A long, dirty journey, bumping up and down on the back of a donkey. Nights along the way sleeping rough, basic food, if any. Fears about the actual delivery - a young girl, not an experienced mother, will it hurt? Will the baby be alright? It might be the son of God but after nine months of intimately knowing this baby your worries would surely have been very human ones.

Then it all started, and although we know little of the obstetric detail or even the actual chain of events, we have a narrative by which we can claim to share in the unfolding miracle.

Holy Mary, Mother of God, your love for mankind, your faithful, selfless devotion to us all is truly awe inspiring and a simple 'Thank you' seems inadequate.

Thank you, I do though, for everything.

With Love.

December 23rd

Fever pitch all day. I have been with some children in a secular holiday creche and mass hysteria is not just something that happens in adult crowds. My ears are still ringing, in fact could be damaged for good and ever, and I am hoarse from singing children's songs and Frosty the Snowman, again and again and again and.................

We had a small story time with a contemporary tale about a young couple, down on their luck and about to have a baby and we asked the older children 4-7 year olds if it sounded like anything else they knew. Surprisingly they all knew the Christmas story and talked about what it must have been like for Mary and Joseph. Then into the earthier realms, as children do, with discussions about how smelly it would have been with all that animal poo around, and would Jesus have been frightened looking up and seeing a cow staring down at him.

One child thought that the presents brought to him were really dangerous and highly unsuitable and wasn't it crazy to give a baby a real-life lamb. 'Yes' said another 'but maybe it meant that he would have some food to eat when they both got a bit bigger.'

Yes, children and Christmas - and the actual story of Christmas, is affirming and the more so for being shared in such a culturally mixed group.

December 24th

Christmas Eve,
We are alone this evening, jut the two of us for a quiet simple supper and
time together before going off to church at 11pm.

O Holy Night, Silent night,
When Angels from the realms of Glory
Swooped over the Hills of the North
Singing Awake, awake, fling off the night
And Hail to the Lords Anointed.
Oh, Little town of Bethlehem
Who is He in Yonder stall at
Whose feet the shepherds fall?
Away in a manger, We will rock you
Whilst Good Christian men Rejoice and carol
O come all Ye Faithful.
While shepherds watched their flocks
A child this day is born, his mother sings
Lully, Lulla thou little tiny child.
Of the Father's love begotten
Holy, holy, holy, Lord God Almighty
Early in the morning our song shall rise to thee.

Happy Christmas Morn.

December 25th

After all the planning and cooking, the day took care of itself. Children were filled with excitement, crisps and chocolate, all before dinner of course and adults were rendered relaxed with various glasses of warming amber nectar to help them relinquish responsibility for a few hours. After dinner, we relaxed into a well fed heap of bodies on the sofa to watch 'The Sound of Music' - again.

All rather different from the Christmas day 1668 in the Pepys household where Samuel wrote:

'Christmas day. To dinner alone with my wife, who, poor wretch! Sat undressed all day, til ten at night, altering and lacing of her noble petticoat: while I by her, making the boy read to me the life of Julius Cæsar, and Des Cartes book of Musick.'

Happy Christmas?

December 26th

Angel voices ever singing
round thy throne of light,
Angel harps for ever ringing
rest not day nor night,
Thousands only live to bless thee
and confess thee
Lord of might.
Honour, glory, might and merit
thine shall ever be,
Father, Son and Holy Spirit
blessed Trinity.
Of the best that thou hast given
earth and heaven
render thee.

General Assembly of the Presbyterian Church of the USA

December 27th

Angel voices must be raising the roof, the strings of lights decorating earth
are nothing compared to the light around the throne of God.
Lord of might, of power, coming as a human baby to show us all how our
relationship with you is one of total dependence and yet how we become
the babe and you the father, asking us to trust, to depend, to rely on you.
Yea, we know that thou rejoicest
o'er each work of thine;
Thou didst ears and hands and voices
for thy praise design;
craftsman's art and music's measure
for thy pleasure
all combine.
      Amen

December 28th

We are going away to celebrate the New Year with friends in Wiltshire, such dear friends that it is really like going home. We all seem to just fit, like a comfy cardigan, giving warmth and comfort with no straining or rough edges, like a soft cashmere blanket wrapped round, not to smother or restrain but to envelop one in the luxury of care and attention.

We need to learn to take as well as give. Taking with grace gives the giver the opportunity to feel valued and appreciated and I am going to allow myself much cossetting for the next few days.

December 29th

We had a leisurely drive down from Cambridge yesterday, stopping for lunch en route and stretching our legs with a short walk that we know along the banks of the river Windrush. It was not very inspiring weather but it really didn't matter, we chatted about Christmas and the joy of the children and their children, of the dogs pushing for space in front of the fire, of our appreciation for our continuing health and our anticipation at seeing our pals.

As expected we were 'home from home' the second we arrived and eventually stopped talking at about quarter to midnight, when, full of supper, a glass or two of wine and much laughter we climbed the stairs.

We call ourselves brothers and sisters in Christ, which we are and yet we don't need nomenclature to say 'dear friends, we love you'.

December 30th

We are going to walk today and then this evening we are going to visit some other folks, friends of our friends, for dinner and to see in the New Year. I'm always rather melancholy on this night and every year it seems to get a little heavier.
I thought about a couple of lines from the wonderful Dylan Thomas poem as another year is coming to its close:
'Do not go gentle into that good night,
Rage, Rage, against the dying of the light.'

Tempus fugit, to darned fast for my liking.

December 31st

The Lord Bless you and keep you.
The Lord make His face to shine upon you,
To shine upon you and be gracious unto you,
The Lord bless you and keep you,
The Lord turn His face towards you and
Give you His Peace.

Numbers 6: 24-26

Amen

Notes

www.ingramcontent.com/pod-product-compliance
Lightning Source LLC
La Vergne TN
LVHW051509080426
835509LV00017B/2001